Mornings
with
GOD

My Daily
Prayer Journal

Mornings
with
GOD

My Daily
Prayer Journal

EMILY BIGGERS & VICKIE PHELPS

BARBOUR BOOKS
An Imprint of Barbour Publishing, Inc.

ISBN 978-1-64352-627-0

Published by Barbour Books, an imprint of Barbour Publishing, Inc., 1810 Barbour Drive, Uhrichsville, Ohio 44683, www.barbourbooks.com

Our mission is to inspire the world with the life-changing message of the Bible.

Member of the
Evangelical Christian
Publishers Association

Printed in China.

As women seeking to live out our faith in a busy world, we simply must begin each day in the presence of God. He longs to make Himself known to us. *Mornings with God* is a collection of prayers, scriptures, and brief devotions to help you start each morning with the Lord. As you read the prayer selections, make them your own. Meditate on the scriptures. Record your personal thoughts. God loves you, and He desires daily fellowship with you. You are a daughter of the King of kings. Begin each morning with your Father.

And in the morning, rising up a great
while before day, he went out,
and departed into a solitary place,
and there prayed.
MARK 1:35

DAY 1

Joy Comes in the Morning

*Good morning, God! How many nights will I cry myself to sleep
before I remember that Your Word promises joy when I wake?
In the darkness of the night, my troubles seem insurmountable.
But they're not. Everything seems fresh in the morning. I realize
once again that together, we can do this. Thank You, Father,
for a new day! May I discover true joy in it. Amen.*

When worry overwhelms you in the darkness, trust what God has shown
you to be true in the light. Each day His mercies are new!

*Weeping may endure for a night,
but joy cometh in the morning.*

PSALM 30:5

DAY 2

Fresh Joy

Lord, thank You for giving me a clean, fresh slate today. I can start anew. Yesterday's mistakes are behind me. I can begin again, knowing that You will be with me each step of the way. Your Word reminds me that You are the same every day. You won't give up on me or hold the failures of the past against me. Thank You for always being the same. Amen.

Don't allow mistakes of the past to hold you captive in their prison. When others remind you of your failures, remember that Jesus never changes and He will free you from the prison of the past.

Jesus Christ the same yesterday, and to day, and for ever.

HEBREWS 13:8

DAY 3
The Joy of the Lord

Lord, some mornings I wake up ready to go! I feel rested and energetic. Other mornings, I wonder how I will make it through the day. Remind me that as Your child, I have a power source that is always available to me. I may not always feel joyful, but the joy of the Lord is my strength. As I spend time in Your Word, renew my strength, I pray. In Jesus' name, amen.

Those who read and meditate upon the Word of the Lord know His heart in a unique way. True joy comes through a relationship with the Father.

....

....

....

....

....

....

....

....

....

....

....

For the joy of the Lord is your strength.
NEHEMIAH 8:10

Where Did My Joy Go?

Lord, some days I feel like my joy has seeped out. The cares of life have crept in and poked holes in my heart, and without my realizing it, I've lost the joy I felt each day. Please restore unto me the joy of my salvation. Help me to resist the urge to give in to disappointments and failures. In Jesus' name, I ask it. Amen.

Sometimes we get caught up in all that life demands of us and we forget to be joyful. Our joy seeps out. The psalmist David asked the Lord to restore his joy. Ask Him to do the same for you.

....

....

....

....

....

....

....

....

....

....

*Restore unto me the joy of thy salvation;
and uphold me with thy free spirit.*

PSALM 51:12

True Joy

Thank You, Father, for Your Word, which teaches me how to experience true joy. This world sends me a lot of messages through the media and through those that do not know You. I have tried some of the things that are supposed to bring joy, but they always leave me empty in the end. Thank You for the truth. Help me to abide in You, that I might be overflowing with joy. Amen.

Did you realize that Jesus Christ wants you to be *full* of joy? Even *overflowing* with joy? Read John 15, which teaches how to be joy filled.

These things have I spoken unto you, that my joy might remain in you, and that your joy might be full.

JOHN 15:11

DAY 6
Joy in Small Things

*Father, help me to find joy in the small things I experience
each day. I don't want to take for granted what You have provided
for me. Open my eyes that I may see all that You are doing in my world
on a day-to-day basis. No matter what is happening around me,
help me to take joy in this day that You've created. Amen.*

God has created this day for us, His creation. Why shouldn't we rejoice that we know the Creator personally and He has made another day in which we can take joy?

....

....

....

....

....

....

....

....

....

....

*This is the day which the LORD hath made;
we will rejoice and be glad in it.*

PSALM 118:24

Joyful in Hope

God, the longer I live, the more I realize that joy and hope go hand in hand. I have joy because my hope is in You. Thank You, Lord, that as Your daughter, I do not go out to face the day in hopelessness. No matter what happens, I can find joy because my hope is not in this world or in my circumstances. My hope is in the Lord. Amen.

Those that trust in the name of the Lord are set apart. There is joy in the countenance of a believer that does not shine forth from the face of the hopeless.

Happy is he that hath the God of Jacob for his help, whose hope is in the LORD his God.

PSALM 146:5

A Strong Tower

*Father, the longer I know You, the more grateful I am that I can
run to You with all my problems, my desires, even my deepest longing.
All I have to do is speak Your name and I can find strength for each
day. I come now, calling upon Your name, knowing that the tower
of strength I need will be there for me. In the name of Jesus, amen.*

When we speak the name of Jesus, we are speaking life, hope, and
strength into every situation we are facing. What are you facing today?
Speak His name and you will find help and a tower of safety.

*The name of the LORD is a strong tower:
the righteous runneth into it, and is safe.*
PROVERBS 18:10

DAY 9
Joy in the Name of the Lord

Father, this morning I meet You here for just a few moments before the busyness of the day takes over. I trust You. It is not always easy to trust, but You have proven trustworthy in my life. I find joy in the knowledge that You are my Defender. You go before me this day into battle. I choose joy today because I love the name of the Lord Almighty. Amen.

What joy there is in this: if you are a daughter of the Sovereign God, you never have to wonder if He will be there for you. He is trustworthy.

But let all those that put their trust in thee rejoice:
let them ever shout for joy, because thou defendest them:
let them also that love thy name be joyful in thee.

PSALM 5:11

DAY 10
Living a Godly Life

Father, I want to live a godly life that pleases You. I want to be a light to others in my path. Sometimes I make decisions that don't reflect that kind of lifestyle. As I go through each day, help me to consider my choices and whether they are pleasing to You and a witness to other people. I want to be one of those You set apart. Amen.

Godly living pleases God. Living for ourselves separates us from Him and others. When our life pleases God, then He hears our prayers when we call on Him.

But know that the Lord hath set apart him that is godly for himself: the Lord will hear when I call unto him.

PSALM 4:3

Joyful Regardless of Circumstances

Lord, there are days when I can't help but rejoice in what You are doing. But many times the daily grind is just rather humdrum. There is nothing to rejoice about, much less give thanks for! Or is there? Help me, Father, to be joyful and thankful every day. Each day is a gift from You. Remind me of this truth today, and give me a joyful, thankful heart, I ask. Amen.

Do you know someone who is always wearing a smile? That individual has made a choice to be joyful regardless of circumstances. *Choose to have a joyful, thankful attitude.*

Rejoice evermore. Pray without ceasing. In every thing give thanks: for this is the will of God in Christ Jesus concerning you.

1 Thessalonians 5:16–18

Do Good

Lord, sometimes I'm not as kind as I need to be. Some days I find it hard to go out of my way to speak to others or show them consideration. It's not their fault. The fault lies with me. Sometimes I'm just having a bad day or maybe I don't feel well, but help me to put aside my feelings and show Your love and compassion to those around me regardless of how I feel. Amen.

Is there someone you need to speak to today? Someone who needs to see your smile or feel kindness from you? Ask the Lord to give you a sweet spirit as you go through your day.

_____

_____

_____

_____

_____

_____

_____

_____

*Withhold not good from them to whom it is due,
when it is in the power of thine hand to do it.*
PROVERBS 3:27

Joyful in Song

Heavenly Father, this morning I come to You with a song on my lips and joy in my heart. I thank You for all that You are doing in my life. You are at work when I sense Your presence and even when I don't. I praise You for being God. I rejoice because I am Your daughter. Amen.

The Bible speaks of rejoicing with song, praising God through music, and even dancing before the Lord. How will you praise your heavenly Father today through music?

....

....

....

....

....

....

....

....

The LORD is my strength and my shield; my heart trusted in him, and I am helped: therefore my heart greatly rejoiceth; and with my song will I praise him.

PSALM 28:7

A Promise

Jesus, when You were here on earth, You performed great miracles. Before You returned to the Father, You gave Your followers and those who believe on You a great promise. We would do the same works You did and even more. Help me to embrace that promise, believe it, and trust You to bring about those greater works through my life. Amen.

Is there something the Lord wants to do through you? Do you feel His gentle nudge encouraging you to work for Him? Step out by faith and embrace the promise of greater works.

....

....

....

....

....

....

....

....

....

....

Verily, verily, I say unto you, He that believeth on me, the works that I do shall he do also; and greater works than these shall he do; because I go unto my Father.

JOHN 14:12

No More Sorrow

*Jesus, Your disciples were dismayed. You told them You were going
away but that You would see them again. Those men had walked
and talked with You. You were their leader, their friend. How lost
they must have felt at Your crucifixion! But three days later. . .
Wow! Lord, You turn mourning into rejoicing. Help me
to trust in this. Thank You, Jesus. Amen.*

Today your heart may be heavy with loss or longing. One day there will
be no more sorrow, only joy! Claim this promise from God's Word.

*And ye now therefore have sorrow: but I will see you again,
and your heart shall rejoice, and your joy no man taketh from you.*
JOHN 16:22

Walk in the Spirit

Lord, sometimes I let the flesh rule in my life, whether it's spending too much money, speaking when I need to keep quiet, or spreading gossip. Maybe it's not a big temptation, just things that aren't good for me as a woman or a Christian. Show me how to walk in the Spirit day by day that I won't fulfill the lusts of the flesh. Help me to be attentive to the Spirit. Amen.

When the small, still voice of the Holy Spirit speaks, listen. He will lead you in the right direction, helping you to live in a way that pleases God.

This I say then, Walk in the Spirit, and ye shall not fulfil the lust of the flesh.

Galatians 5:16

DAY 17
Joy in God's Word

Thank You, God, that in Your holy scriptures I find the ways of life.
I find wise counsel on the pages of my Bible. You reveal the truth
to me, Lord, and there is no greater blessing than to know the
truth. You tell me in Your Word that the truth sets me free.
I am free to live a life that brings You glory and honor.
May others see the joy I have found in You! Amen.

God may not write the answers to your questions in the sky, but they are written on the pages of His timeless, truth-filled Word.

_____

_____

_____

_____

_____

_____

_____

_____

_____

_____

Thou hast made known to me the ways of life;
thou shalt make me full of joy with thy countenance.
ACTS 2:28

Leaping to Victory

Father, some weeks are tough ones. It seems that everything that could go wrong, did. I know Your servant David went through some very rough times, but he acknowledged that it was by Your help that he conquered every foe. Help me to claim that same victory through Your power. In myself, I can do nothing, but I can make it with Your help. Amen.

You may feel as though you've been attacked unmercifully. Discouragement may be nipping at your heels. Take courage; with God on your side, you can leap over those obstacles.

For by thee I have run through a troop;
and by my God have I leaped over a wall.

PSALM 18:29

Glorifying God in My Work

God, today as I work both in my home and outside of it, may my attitude glorify You. I am not of this world, but I am in it, and often it has too much influence on me. May I think twice before I grumble, Father, about the tasks set before me this day. I will choose to work as unto my Father, and may my countenance reflect Your love to those around me. Amen.

God ordained that mankind should work and then rest. He modeled this for us in His creation of the world. Work. . .because God calls us to do so.

....

....

....

....

....

....

....

....

And whatsoever ye do, do it heartily, as to the Lord, and not unto men; knowing that of the Lord ye shall receive the reward of the inheritance: for ye serve the Lord Christ.

COLOSSIANS 3:23–24

Soft Answers

Lord, sometimes my words are harsh. I don't mean to speak that way, but often they come out sounding grumpy or angry. Show me how to speak soft answers that will encourage and comfort those around me. Help me to slow down and think about what I'm going to say instead of speaking in anger. Amen.

What kind of words are you speaking today? Do you feel angry, frustrated, or discouraged? Ask God to help you slow down and think about what you're going to say so your words don't make the situation worse.

_____

_____

_____

_____

_____

_____

_____

_____

A soft answer turneth away wrath: but grievous words stir up anger. The tongue of the wise useth knowledge aright: but the mouth of fools poureth out foolishness.

PROVERBS 15:1–2

Serve One Another

God, I have not been put on this earth to serve myself. It is not all about me. Sometimes I forget that! Service is what this life is all about, isn't it? Father, give me opportunities to show love to others today. Make every moment a "God moment." Help me to be aware of the many needs around me. Create in me a heart that loves others and puts them ahead of myself. Amen.

Consider your motive for service. Are you serving others because you want to be noticed for your kindness? Or are you serving others in love and true compassion?

_____

_____

_____

_____

_____

_____

_____

_____

For, brethren, ye have been called unto liberty; only use not liberty for an occasion to the flesh, but by love serve one another. For all the law is fulfilled in one word, even in this; Thou shalt love thy neighbour as thyself.

GALATIANS 5:13–14

Press Forward

Jesus, I know You have forgiven me of my past. You have made me clean, but Satan would like me to believe that those things are still against me. Help me to put those things behind me and press on to the life You want me to live. Amen.

Don't listen to Satan. He is a liar and will discourage you and bring you down if you allow it. Forget those things in the past, and press forward in Christ.

....

....

....

....

....

....

....

....

....

Brethren, I count not myself to have apprehended: but this one thing I do, forgetting those things which are behind, and reaching forth unto those things which are before, I press toward the mark for the prize of the high calling of God in Christ Jesus.

PHILIPPIANS 3:13–14

DAY 23
Opportunities to Serve

Father, with this new day, give me new eyes. Show me the hungry,
the lonely, the tired. Show me those who need encouragement,
those who need a friend, those who need to see Jesus in me.
I don't want to miss the chances that You give me to be a blessing
to others. I know that when I serve others, the heart of my Creator
is blessed. Make me aware of others' needs, I ask. Amen.

Today offer a smile or a hug. Give away your time, talents, or resources.
It will come back to you tenfold in the blessing you receive for serving
others.

....
....
....
....
....
....
....

And the King shall answer and say unto them, Verily I say
unto you, Inasmuch as ye have done it unto one of the
least of these my brethren, ye have done it unto me.
Matthew 25:40

DAY 24

Don't Be Shaken

Father, there are many voices and influences in the world all vying for my attention. I feel pulled in many directions. Help me to sit quietly and wait for Your voice to lead me down the right path. Don't let the influence of the world shake my faith or cause me to get off track as I await Your soon return. Amen.

Are you being influenced by the world and its trends? Be still before God and listen to His voice. He will keep you from falling prey to the enemy's tactics.

···

···

···

···

···

···

···

···

···

Now we beseech you, brethren, by the coming of our Lord Jesus Christ, and by our gathering together unto him, that ye be not soon shaken in mind, or be troubled, neither by spirit, nor by word, nor by letter as from us, as that the day of Christ is at hand.

2 THESSALONIANS 2:1–2

Putting God First

*Father, a glance at my bank statement causes me to shudder.
Where does my money go? Am I too concerned with what the world
says I must possess to be cool, to fit in, to appear successful?
Your Word says that I cannot serve both material wealth
and You. I choose You, Lord. Be the Master of my life
and of my checkbook. I need Your help with this. Amen.*

God knows this world sends you a lot of messages. He understands temptation. Call on Him to help you make wise financial decisions. Put Him first, and He will provide all that you need.

*No man can serve two masters: for either he will hate
the one, and love the other; or else he will hold to the one,
and despise the other. Ye cannot serve God and mammon.*
MATTHEW 6:24

DAY 26
Have Faith

Lord, why is it harder to believe for some things more than others? Why do I have faith that some things will be taken care of and waffle about things that might seem harder? Help my unbelief. Give me the faith to believe that You can do whatever needs to be done in any given situation. Nothing is too hard for You. Amen.

Like the woman with the issue of blood, we need to touch Jesus. Reach out to Him today, and in faith, believe that He can meet any need in your life, big or little.

And he said unto her, Daughter, thy faith hath made thee whole; go in peace, and be whole of thy plague.

MARK 5:34

Showing Mercy

Jesus, like the Good Samaritan in Your parable, may I too show mercy. Some may never enter the doors of a church, but what a difference an act of grace could make! Put before me opportunities to show unmerited favor. That is, after all, what You have shown to me. You died for my sins. I could never have earned salvation. It is a free gift, an act of grace. Make me merciful. Amen.

Two other men saw the man who had fallen among thieves. Will you pass by, as they did, when you see someone in need? Or will you show mercy like the Good Samaritan?

....

....

....

....

....

....

....

....

Which now of these three, thinkest thou, was neighbour unto him that fell among the thieves? And he said, He that shewed mercy on him. Then said Jesus unto him, Go, and do thou likewise.

LUKE 10:36–37

Lift Up My Head

Lord, there are days when my spirit is so low that my head hangs down and my smile disappears. I can't seem to look up because I'm weighted down with problems. When I feel this way, only You can help me. Lift up my head today, Lord. Open my eyes to see You in all Your glory. Help me to know that You are with me in every situation. Amen.

Are you weighted down with problems today? Are you surrounded by situations that overwhelm you? Call out to God. He is your shield. He will lift up your head and ease your load.

....

....

....

....

....

....

....

....

....

....

But thou, O LORD, art a shield for me;
my glory, and the lifter up of mine head.
PSALM 3:3

What Would Jesus Do?

Heavenly Father, sometimes I am a Sunday Christian. How I want to worship You with the rest of my week! Please help me to be mindful of You throughout the week. May Your will and Your ways permeate my thoughts and decisions. Whether I am taking care of things at home or working with others in the workplace, may I glorify You in all that I say and do. Amen.

As you go about your daily activities, remember the Lord. Do everything with Him in mind. WWJD: *What would Jesus do?*

_____

_____

_____

_____

_____

_____

_____

_____

Whether therefore ye eat, or drink,
or whatsoever ye do, do all to the glory of God.
1 CORINTHIANS 10:31

Spirit of Meekness

Jesus, help me not to criticize others when they get involved in the wrong thing. I need to remember that I'm not perfect either. We're all subject to temptation. It's only by Your grace that I make it. Help me to have a meek spirit and reach out to the one who needs to be restored. Remind me that without You, I can be caught up in the same situation. Amen.

When others make a mistake, pray for them instead of whispering about them. Consider the fact that we can all be tempted to get into the wrong thing if we're not careful.

Brethren, if a man be overtaken in a fault, ye which are spiritual, restore such an one in the spirit of meekness; considering thyself, lest thou also be tempted.

GALATIANS 6:1

Use Me, Lord

Savior, You laid down Your life for me. You died a horrible death upon a cross. It was death by crucifixion, which was reserved for the worst of criminals. And You had done nothing wrong. You came into the world to save us! You gave Your very life for us. Jesus, take my life. Use me for Your kingdom's work. Only in losing my life for You will I save it. Amen.

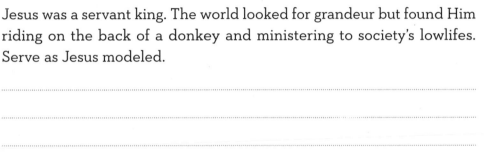

Jesus was a servant king. The world looked for grandeur but found Him riding on the back of a donkey and ministering to society's lowlifes. Serve as Jesus modeled.

For whosoever will save his life shall lose it; but whosoever shall lose his life for my sake and the gospel's, the same shall save it.

MARK 8:35

Walk Worthy

Lord, teach me how to walk with You each day. Help me to live and follow a path worthy of Your calling on my life. As a Christian, my life should glorify You and be a blessing to others. Help me not to do anything that would bring reproach on You or Your kingdom. Amen.

Paul instructed the Ephesian Christians to walk worthy of their vocation. Living a life that glorifies God is important to our vocation as a Christian.

I therefore, the prisoner of the Lord, beseech you that ye walk worthy of the vocation wherewith ye are called, with all lowliness and meekness, with longsuffering, forbearing one another in love; endeavouring to keep the unity of the Spirit in the bond of peace.

Ephesians 4:1-3

DAY 33

A Giving Heart

Father, may I be honest? Sometimes I don't feel like serving. They keep asking if I will help with this or that at church. And there is always a collection being taken up. Can't I just focus on me? I have my own needs! But oh, the peace I feel when I lay my head on my pillow at night knowing I have loved with action, with sacrifice. Make me a giver, I ask. Amen.

The very richest people in the world are those that give it all away. There is a joy in generosity that the stingy forfeit with every coin saved.

Remember the words of the Lord Jesus, how he said, It is more blessed to give than to receive.

ACTS 20:35

One Spirit

Jesus, let me stand with my Christian sisters as one in the Spirit.
Help me not to be self-centered, always wanting things my way.
We're all striving together for Your kingdom. Help us to
stand fast together that we will be pleasing to You
and be ready for Your return. Amen.

Cultivate the relationship you have with other Christian women. Encourage one another in your walk as you strive together for the faith of the Gospel. Learn to speak words that edify each one in the group.

Only let your conversation be as it becometh the gospel of Christ:
that whether I come and see you, or else be absent, I may hear
of your affairs, that ye stand fast in one spirit, with one
mind striving together for the faith of the gospel.

PHILIPPIANS 1:27

Glorifying God

Father, I tend to seek the glory for myself. It is human nature, I know, but I want to be different. I am Your daughter. Let me shine, and when others ask me, "Why the smile?" or "Why the good deeds?" let me point them to You. You are the source of all that is good in me. You have given me each ability I have. May I reflect Your love through my good works. Amen.

Always point others to your heavenly Father when they notice you. There is nothing good in you without Him.

Let your light so shine before men, that they may see your good works, and glorify your Father which is in heaven.

MATTHEW 5:16

Acceptable Words

Lord, I'm sorry for the harsh words I spoke in anger. I'm sorry for dwelling on thoughts that cause me to speak in such a way. Forgive me, and help me to remember that my words can hurt someone deeply. Not only do I hurt others, but You hear me when I speak. You know the intent of my heart. Help me to speak only words that are acceptable to You. Amen.

Are there words you wish you hadn't spoken? Words you want to take back, but now it's too late? Weigh your words carefully before you speak them. Ask God to give you acceptable words.

_____

_____

_____

_____

_____

_____

_____

_____

Let the words of my mouth, and the meditation of my heart, be acceptable in thy sight, O LORD, my strength, and my redeemer.

PSALM 19:14

Honoring My Parents

Heavenly Father, show me how to honor my parents. Even as I have grown into a woman, Your command remains. Give me patience with my parents. Remind me that with age comes wisdom. Help me to seek their counsel when it is appropriate. God, in Your sovereignty, You gave me the mother and father that You did. May I honor You as I honor them. Amen.

Honoring your parents looks different at four, fourteen, and forty, but this is a lifelong duty and privilege. God is pleased when you honor those that have filled parental roles in your life.

_____

_____

_____

_____

_____

_____

_____

*Honour thy father and thy mother, as the L*ORD *thy God hath commanded thee; that thy days may be prolonged, and that it may go well with thee, in the land which the L*ORD *thy God giveth thee.*

DEUTERONOMY 5:16

Forgive One Another

Father, I need to forgive someone for the hurt they caused me, but the pain is very fresh and I can't even think about the situation or the other person without crying. Please help me to have a forgiving spirit. Just as You have shown me grace and forgiven me, show me how to extend grace to this person so I can forgive them. Amen.

Are you hurting today because of careless words or the thoughtless actions of another person? Thank God for showing you His grace and forgiveness, then ask Him to give you grace to forgive the person who hurt you. Forgiveness brings peace and lightens your load.

....

....

....

....

....

....

....

....

Forbearing one another, and forgiving one another, if any man have a quarrel against any: even as Christ forgave you, so also do ye.
COLOSSIANS 3:13

A Choice to Serve God

Father, it is a daily choice. Will I serve the world? Myself? Or my God?
What will I model for the children in my life who look up to me?
Will my family and friends know me as one who is self-serving or
kingdom-focused? Today I make the choice to serve the Lord.
Help me to truly live as Your servant in this world. Amen.

As a woman, the choices you make often impact your entire family. Choose
to serve the Lord, that your influence might be godly rather than worldly.

As for me and my house, we will serve the LORD.

JOSHUA 24:15

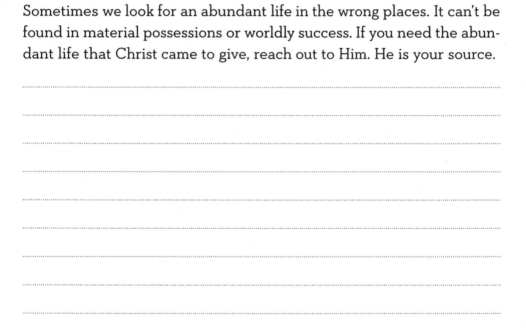

DAY 40

Abundant Life

Jesus, You came that I might have abundant life, but some days my life seems filled with chaos and stress. How can I live an abundant life in the middle of all these problems? Forgive me for complaining, but I need help to live the life You have planned for me. Show me how to live out each day in the abundance that You have provided. Amen.

Sometimes we look for an abundant life in the wrong places. It can't be found in material possessions or worldly success. If you need the abundant life that Christ came to give, reach out to Him. He is your source.

The thief cometh not, but for to steal, and to kill, and to destroy: I am come that they might have life, and that they might have it more abundantly.

JOHN 10:10

Avoiding Idleness

*Lord, I know that You want me to take care of my household.
Sometimes I am so tempted to put off my duties around the house,
and I find myself spending too much time on the computer or the
telephone. Help me to be balanced. Help me to take care of my
household and to be aware of the trap of idleness. I know that
procrastination is not a good or godly habit. Amen.*

Certainly every woman needs some downtime and relaxation, but do
not confuse this with idleness. Idleness is a tool of the devil.

*She looketh well to the ways of her household,
and eateth not the bread of idleness.*

PROVERBS 31:27

Abiding in the Vine

*Jesus, Your Word tells me that You are the vine and I am a branch.
I need to be attached to You to live, but some days, I feel like I've
been broken off the vine and I'm lying on the ground, dead and
dry. Help me to abide in You on a daily basis. That's the only
way I can live and bring forth fruit. I can't do anything
without You. Keep me attached to You. Amen.*

Has your branch been severed from the vine? Without Jesus, you will
wither and die. Ask Him to graft you back onto the vine. Without Him,
you can do nothing.

*I am the vine, ye are the branches: He that abideth in me, and I in him,
the same bringeth forth much fruit: for without me ye can do nothing.*

JOHN 15:5

Every Good Gift

*Father, thank You for the blessings You have poured out on my family.
Often I dwell on that which we do not have. Please remind me to be
ever grateful for so many gifts. The comforts we enjoy each day,
like running water and electricity, are so easily taken for granted.
Thank You for Your provision in our lives. Help me to have a thankful
heart so that my family might be more thankful also. Amen.*

Sometimes making a list of all the things you are thankful for is a good
way to count your blessings. How has God blessed your family?

_____

_____

_____

_____

_____

_____

_____

_____

*And thou shalt rejoice in every good thing which the LORD
thy God hath given unto thee, and unto thine house, thou,
and the Levite, and the stranger that is among you.*

DEUTERONOMY 26:11

Songs of Deliverance

*Father, sometimes I go to the wrong person for help. I need to run
to You when I'm in trouble. Human help is limited, but You can preserve
me from trouble. You can show me the right direction to take. You can
give me a song to sing even in the middle of a bad situation.
Thank You for surrounding me with songs of deliverance. Amen.*

Even though we all need our family and friends, they are limited in their
help for us. God is our hiding place when we're in trouble, and when
everything looks dark, He will give you a song to sing.

*Thou art my hiding place; thou shalt preserve me from trouble;
thou shalt compass me about with songs of deliverance. Selah.*

PSALM 32:7

DAY 45
A God-Centered Home

Father, so many homes are shaken in these days. So many families are shattering to pieces around me. Protect my home, I pray. Protect my loved ones. Be the foundation of my home, strong and solid, consistent and wise. May every decision made here reflect Your principles. May those who visit this home and encounter this family be keenly aware of our uniqueness, because we serve the one true and almighty God. Amen.

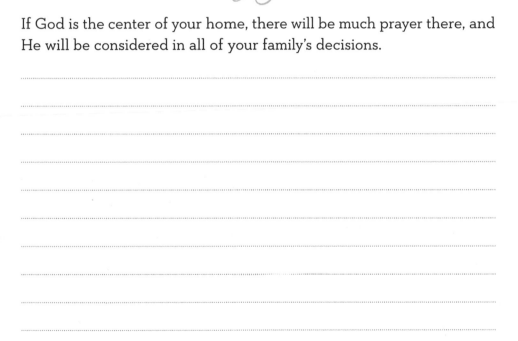

If God is the center of your home, there will be much prayer there, and He will be considered in all of your family's decisions.

Except the LORD build the house, they labour in vain that build it: except the LORD keep the city, the watchman waketh but in vain.

PSALM 127:1

Nothing Can Separate

Jesus, the devil would like me to believe that You don't care about me. He's been whispering those thoughts into my mind, trying to convince me that I might as well give up and go my own way. I know You died for me because You love me. Give me victory over those thoughts, and give me the determination I need to serve You. Amen.

Don't allow the devil to talk to you. Listen for God's voice, and follow His leading. Nothing can separate you from His love.

_____

_____

_____

_____

_____

_____

_____

_____

_____

For I am persuaded, that neither death, nor life, nor angels, nor principalities, nor powers, nor things present, nor things to come, nor height, nor depth, nor any other creature, shall be able to separate us from the love of God, which is in Christ Jesus our Lord.

ROMANS 8:38–39

DAY 47

A Godly Example

God, help me to be an example of a faithful disciple of Christ to my family and friends. Those who are close in our lives have the ability to lead us toward or away from righteousness and godliness. I pray that all I do and say will honor You and that I will never be a stumbling block to others. May all within my sphere of influence find me faithful to You. Amen.

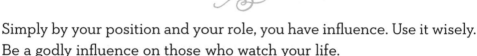

Simply by your position and your role, you have influence. Use it wisely. Be a godly influence on those who watch your life.

The righteous is more excellent than his neighbour: but the way of the wicked seduceth them.

PROVERBS 12:26

Behave Wisely

Father, sometimes I don't use wisdom. David was only a shepherd boy who became a great warrior and a king, but he acted in a wise manner, and as a result, he pleased You and others around him. Help me to behave wisely in all my ways so I can please You. Amen.

God has an abundant supply of wisdom. He can help you to behave wisely at all times. All you have to do is ask.

....

....

....

....

....

....

....

....

....

....

....

....

And David behaved himself wisely in all his ways; and the LORD was with him. Wherefore when Saul saw that he behaved himself very wisely, he was afraid of him. But all Israel and Judah loved David, because he went out and came in before them.

1 SAMUEL 18:14–16

The Value of Fellowship

Heavenly Father, I pray that You will not allow me to isolate myself. I need fellowship with other believers. I benefit from spending time with my Christian friends. You tell us in Your Word that it is not good to be alone. We need one another as we walk through this life with all of its ups and downs. When I am tempted to distance myself from others, guide me back into Christian fellowship. Amen.

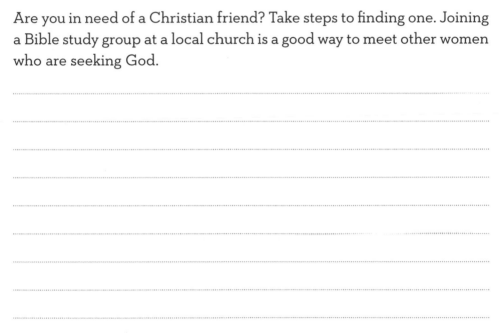

Are you in need of a Christian friend? Take steps to finding one. Joining a Bible study group at a local church is a good way to meet other women who are seeking God.

Two are better than one; because they have a good reward for their labour. For if they fall, the one will lift up his fellow: but woe to him that is alone when he falleth; for he hath not another to help him up.

ECCLESIASTES 4:9-10

Choose to Do Good

Father, forgive me for wanting revenge. Even though my enemy wants to destroy me or my character, help me not to reward evil for evil. When David had a chance to do Saul harm, he knew in his heart that he could not do wrong. He chose to do the right thing. Help me to follow David's example. Amen.

Revenge belongs to God, not us. Let Him take care of the matter.

And it came to pass afterward, that David's heart smote him, because he had cut off Saul's skirt. And he said unto his men, The LORD forbid that I should do this thing unto my master, the LORD's anointed, to stretch forth mine hand against him, seeing he is the anointed of the LORD.

1 SAMUEL 24:5–6

Iron Sharpens Iron

Lord, I find it hard to talk to my friends about areas of their lives in which they are not honoring You. And I certainly do not always appreciate their correction in my life! Father, allow such sweet, godly fellowship between my Christian sisters and me that when truth should be spoken in love, we are able to speak into one another's lives. We need one another. Iron sharpens iron. Amen.

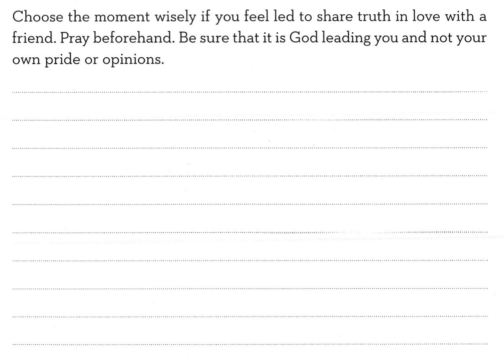

Choose the moment wisely if you feel led to share truth in love with a friend. Pray beforehand. Be sure that it is God leading you and not your own pride or opinions.

Iron sharpeneth iron; so a man sharpeneth the countenance of his friend.

PROVERBS 27:17

A Precious Gift

Thank You, Jesus, for the precious gift of salvation, for redeeming me when I was unworthy. No other gift or possession can be compared to what You have done for the world in offering Your life as a sacrifice. Nothing I have is worth more than this. Help me to keep my priorities in order, and never let me place material possessions above You. Amen.

Do you find yourself caught up in material abundance? In the end, nothing will save you except the blood of Jesus. Nothing is more precious.

They that trust in their wealth, and boast themselves in the multitude of their riches; none of them can by any means redeem his brother, nor give to God a ransom for him: (for the redemption of their soul is precious, and it ceaseth for ever.)

PSALM 49:6–8

Resisting the Urge to Gossip

*Father, men don't seem to struggle with gossip the way we ladies do.
A juicy tidbit of information is so tempting! I need Your help, Lord,
to resist the temptation to gossip. Your Word warns me of the
dangers of gossip and slander. Strengthen me so that I will not
be a troublemaker but rather a peacemaker. Help me to
resist the urge to listen to or speak gossip. Amen.*

God still considers gossip to be gossip when it is cloaked in phrases such
as "I probably shouldn't say this" and "Bless her heart."

*A froward man soweth strife:
and a whisperer separateth chief friends.*

PROVERBS 16:28

Be a Doer

Lord, how many times have I heard Your Word taught and preached or read it for myself and didn't allow it to change me? Forgive me for my indifference. I didn't realize I was indifferent, but hearing Your Word and going my own way or forgetting what I heard or read shows indifference on my part. Open my ears to hear and my mind to receive what You have to say. Amen.

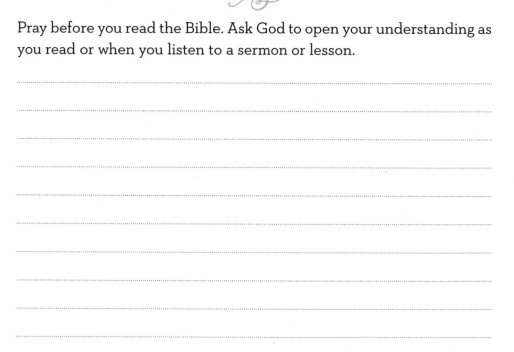

Pray before you read the Bible. Ask God to open your understanding as you read or when you listen to a sermon or lesson.

For if any be a hearer of the word, and not a doer, he is like unto a man beholding his natural face in a glass: for he beholdeth himself, and goeth his way, and straightway forgetteth what manner of man he was.

JAMES 1:23–24

DAY 55
Shield of Faith

God, guard my heart and mind with the shield of faith. I will call on the name of Jesus when Satan tempts me. I will fight against his schemes to ruin me. My weapon is my knowledge of Your Word, promises memorized and cherished. My defense is my faith in Jesus Christ, my Savior. On this faith I will stand. Increase my faith and protect me from the evil one, I pray. Amen.

Satan is alive and well, but he cannot defeat those whose faith in Christ is solid and sure. He is helpless against it.

Above all, taking the shield of faith, wherewith ye shall be able to quench all the fiery darts of the wicked.

Ephesians 6:16

Ready to Answer

*Jesus, help me to be ready to answer questions when someone asks
me what I believe. Plant in me a seed of desire to know more about
You and Your Word. I need to know You in a more intimate
way. Draw me closer to You. Help me be prepared
to share Your Word with others. Amen.*

Challenge yourself to study God's Word on a regular basis so you can
share it with others and answer their questions.

_____

_____

_____

_____

_____

_____

_____

_____

_____

*But sanctify the Lord God in your hearts: and be ready always
to give an answer to every man that asketh you a reason
of the hope that is in you with meekness and fear.*

1 PETER 3:15

DAY 57
Trust in the Lord

Father, I lean on my own understanding, don't I? Help me to trust that You know what is best. Often I make plans and attempt to figure things out when I should submit it all to You in prayer. Bring to mind, as I sit quietly before You now, the times in the past when You have come through for me. Give me faith for my future, knowing that it is in my Father's hands. Amen.

You will never regret putting God first. Lean into His goodness. He wants to bless you with good gifts. He is your loving Father.

Trust in the LORD with all thine heart; and lean not unto thine own understanding. In all thy ways acknowledge him, and he shall direct thy paths.

PROVERBS 3:5–6

The Things of This World

Father, forgive me for the times when I have allowed the things of this world to distract me and draw me away from You and Your love. I repent of the love that I had for material possessions and the idols and success the world flaunts. Let me love You above everything else. Let my love for You conquer and overcome love for this world. Amen.

Is there anything that distracts you and draws you away from God? Don't allow love for this world to take priority over your relationship with Him.

_____

_____

_____

_____

_____

_____

_____

_____

_____

If ye then be risen with Christ, seek those things which are above, where Christ sitteth on the right hand of God. Set your affection on things above, not on things on the earth.

COLOSSIANS 3:1–2

Things Not Seen

Jesus, it is easy to believe in that which I can see. I wish I could reach out and touch You. As I meditate on Your Word, give me faith in that which I cannot see. Give me faith that all of Your promises are true and that one day You will come again in the clouds to take me home. Amen.

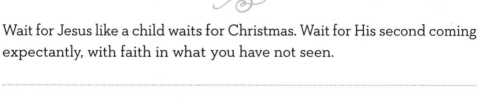

Wait for Jesus like a child waits for Christmas. Wait for His second coming expectantly, with faith in what you have not seen.

Now faith is the substance of things hoped for, the evidence of things not seen.
Hebrews 11:1

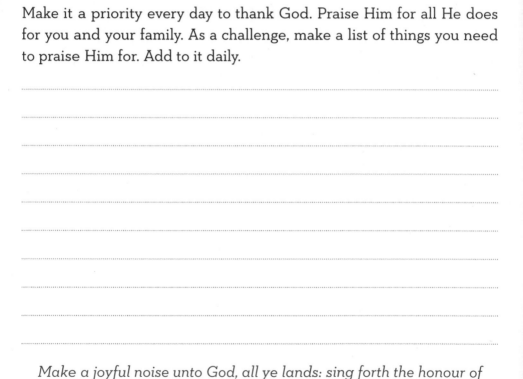

DAY 60
Make His Praise Glorious

*Father, sometimes I forget to thank You for everything You've done
for me. I get too busy, too caught up in my daily life and forget to tell
You how much I appreciate Your goodness to me. Right now, I want
to praise You for Your work in my life. Show me how to be more
grateful for who You are and what You mean to me. Amen.*

Make it a priority every day to thank God. Praise Him for all He does
for you and your family. As a challenge, make a list of things you need
to praise Him for. Add to it daily.

*Make a joyful noise unto God, all ye lands: sing forth the honour of
his name: make his praise glorious. . . . All the earth shall worship thee,
and shall sing unto thee; they shall sing to thy name. Selah.*

PSALM 66:1–2, 4

God Is Faithful

God, I focus a lot on my faith in You. And then You show me that it is not all about me. You are faithful to me. You show me how to be faithful. You never leave. You never give up on me. You never turn away. You always show up. You always believe in me. You are faithful by Your very nature. You cannot be unfaithful. Thank You for Your faithfulness in my life. Amen.

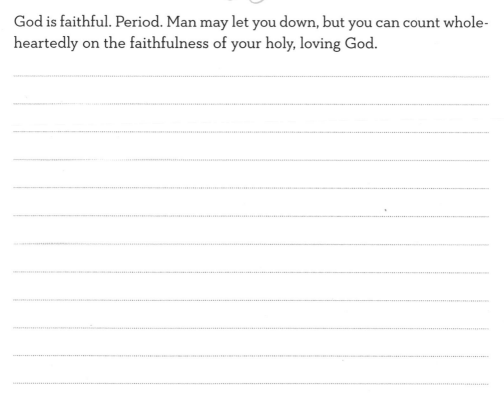

God is faithful. Period. Man may let you down, but you can count wholeheartedly on the faithfulness of your holy, loving God.

But the Lord is faithful, who shall stablish you, and keep you from evil.

2 Thessalonians 3:3

Listen for His Knock

*Jesus, how many times have You knocked at the door of my heart
and I didn't hear You? I was too wrapped up in my own desires and
the busyness of life to realize You were standing outside waiting for
me to open the door. Forgive me. Give me an attentive ear to
hear and a hungry heart to want fellowship with You
more than I want my own desires. Amen.*

Listen for the Savior's knock at your heart's door. He wants to have fellowship with you.

*Behold, I stand at the door, and knock: if any man hear my voice,
and open the door, I will come in to him, and will
sup with him, and he with me.*

REVELATION 3:20

Increase My Faith

*Lord, my faith is small. Thank You for the promise in Your Word that
You can work with even a mustard seed of faith! I submit my lack
of faith to You and ask that You grow and stretch my trust in You.
I want my faith to be great. As I meditate on Your love for me,
please increase my faith that You are sovereign and
You will take care of all my needs. Amen.*

There are many things that man cannot attain, but nothing is impossible
with God. That is why we need faith.

_____

_____

_____

_____

_____

_____

_____

_____

*Verily I say unto you, If ye have faith as a grain of mustard seed,
ye shall say unto this mountain, Remove hence to yonder place;
and it shall remove; and nothing shall be impossible unto you.*

MATTHEW 17:20

A Burning Bush

Father, how many times have You placed a burning bush in my presence as You did for Moses and I didn't bother to find out what You were trying to do? Moses took the time to see why the bush in his life wasn't burned up. Because of that, You did a great work through him. Help me to stop and see what You are trying to accomplish in my life. Amen.

Is there a burning bush in your life? Check it out. God may be trying to do something for you or through you.

....

....

....

....

....

....

....

....

And Moses said, I will now turn aside, and see this great sight, why the bush is not burnt. And when the LORD saw that he turned aside to see, God called unto him out of the midst of the bush, and said, Moses, Moses. And he said, Here am I.

EXODUS 3:3–4

Saved by Grace through Faith

God, it is so comforting to know that my position before You is secure. Thank You for seeing me through a new lens. When You look at me, because I have been saved through faith, You see Your Son in me. You no longer see sin but righteousness. I couldn't have earned it, no matter how hard I worked. Thank You for the gift of salvation through my faith in Jesus. Amen.

A caterpillar, once it becomes a butterfly, can never go back to being a caterpillar. A Christian's position before God is secure upon the profession of faith in Christ.

For by grace are ye saved through faith; and that not of yourselves: it is the gift of God: not of works, lest any man should boast.

EPHESIANS 2:8–9

Meditate on God's Word

Father, help me to meditate on You and Your Word as I go through my day. There are so many things begging for my attention, and it's easy to give in to those thoughts. But You have promised that if we meditate on Your Word and follow its teaching, we will have success. I want to be a successful servant for You and Your work. Amen.

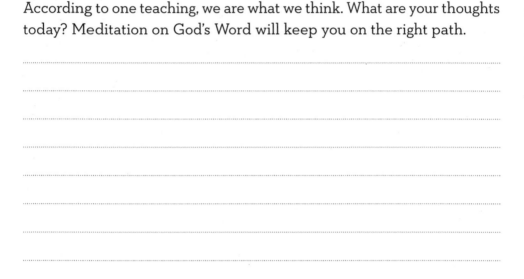

According to one teaching, we are what we think. What are your thoughts today? Meditation on God's Word will keep you on the right path.

....

....

....

....

....

....

....

....

....

....

This book of the law shall not depart out of thy mouth; but thou shalt meditate therein day and night, that thou mayest observe to do according to all that is written therein: for then thou shalt make thy way prosperous, and then thou shalt have good success.

JOSHUA 1:8

Faith Pleases God

Father, I read of Enoch, Noah, Abraham, and Joseph. I know the stories of Sarah and Rahab. The Bible is full of men and women of faith. Those who pleased You were not those who were the wealthiest, most beautiful, or had the most important names. What pleases You, my Father, is faith. Without it, I cannot please You. I choose to live by faith as my spiritual ancestors lived. Strengthen my faith, I ask. Amen.

To know that one cannot please God without faith inspires us to nurture and work out our faith. It is not a thing to be set upon the shelf and forgotten. It must be active and alive.

But without faith it is impossible to please him: for he that cometh to God must believe that he is, and that he is a rewarder of them that diligently seek him.

HEBREWS 11:6

Good Judgment

Lord, teach me how to make good decisions. I don't want to be impulsive and do things without consulting You or others involved. Show me how to think things through so my final decision will be made with wisdom. Teach me knowledge in the situations I face. Help me to live by Your commandments so I will have good judgment. Amen.

❧

When we're impulsive, we sometimes face unpleasant consequences. When we follow God's plan, we will use good judgment and make better decisions.

_____

_____

_____

_____

_____

_____

_____

_____

_____

Teach me good judgment and knowledge: for I have believed thy commandments. Before I was afflicted I went astray: but now have I kept thy word. Thou art good, and doest good; teach me thy statutes.

PSALM 119:66–68

DAY 69
What Is My "Isaac"?

*Heavenly Father, I am amazed by the faith of Abraham. He offered
up his son, Isaac, the one for whom he had waited and waited,
the promised one. When You tested his faith, he answered immediately.
He rose up early in the morning and acted on Your command.
Would I have had the faith that Abraham had in You? Would I trust
You even in my worst nightmare? I hope so. How I hope so. Amen.*

What is the "Isaac" in your life? What would be the most difficult for
you to give up if God were to ask for it? Is it your job? A relationship?
Consider your "Isaac" today.

_____

_____

_____

_____

_____

_____

_____

*By faith Abraham, when he was tried, offered up Isaac: and he
that had received the promises offered up his only begotten son,
of whom it was said, That in Isaac shall thy seed be called:
accounting that God was able to raise him up, even from
the dead; from whence also he received him in a figure.*
HEBREWS 11:17–19

A Mind to Work

*Father, when Nehemiah set out to restore the wall of Jerusalem,
he needed help and the people helped him. Even though they faced
opposition, they got the job done because they had a mind to work.
Give me a mind to work. Help me not to be lazy or nonchalant
about working for You. When You give me a job to
do, help me to get busy and do it. Amen.*

Do you have a mind to work when God has a job for you, or do you let it
ride until you get in the mood to do it? What if God treated us the same
way we treat His requests when He asks something of us?

_____

_____

_____

_____

_____

_____

_____

_____

_____

*So built we the wall; and all the wall was joined together
unto the half thereof: for the people had a mind to work.*

NEHEMIAH 4:6

Praying for Bold Faith

*I desire a bold faith, Jesus. Like the woman who followed You,
crying out, asking that You cast a demon from her daughter.
She was a Gentile, not a Jew; yet, she called You the "Son of David."
She acknowledged You as the Messiah. And You stopped. Her faith
impressed You. You healed the child. May I be so bold. May I recognize
that You are the only solution to every problem. Amen.*

Don't be afraid to go before the throne of God with confidence. You are
His child, saved by the blood of His Son. Have a bold faith!

*Then Jesus answered and said unto her, O woman, great is thy
faith: be it unto thee even as thou wilt. And her daughter
was made whole from that very hour.*

MATTHEW 15:28

A Daily Habit of Praise

Father, thank You for Your goodness to me and my family, for Your faithfulness, which knows no bounds. I want to sing praises to Your name because of Your loving-kindness. Help me not to neglect to praise You every day. With my mouth, my life, and whatever means is available to me, enable me to use that means to give You thanks. Amen.

Do you ever get busy and forget to thank God for His blessings on your life? The Bible says that it's a good thing to give thanks unto the Lord. Make it a daily habit.

It is a good thing to give thanks unto the LORD, and to sing praises unto thy name, O Most High: to shew forth thy lovingkindness in the morning, and thy faithfulness every night, upon an instrument of ten strings, and upon the psaltery; upon the harp with a solemn sound.

PSALM 92:1–3

Trying of My Faith

Father, Your Word tells me that You have begun a good work in me and You will be faithful to complete it. Help me to resist the temptation to sin. I know that it's a process and that no one is perfect, but I desire to grow in my faith. I want to be a faithful daughter of the King. Bless my efforts, Father, and strengthen me as only You can. Amen.

Do you count it as joy when temptations come? That is a tough order. The Lord knows that your faith will not be complete and perfect without trials. Stand firm.

My brethren, count it all joy when ye fall into divers temptations; knowing this, that the trying of your faith worketh patience. But let patience have her perfect work, that ye may be perfect and entire, wanting nothing.

JAMES 1:2–4

Whatever It Takes

Jesus, Zacchaeus wanted to see You so much that he climbed a tree to be able to catch a glimpse of You. He didn't let being short keep him from finding a way to see You. Give me that same determination in my walk with You. Help me to use whatever means available and do whatever it takes to draw closer to You. Amen.

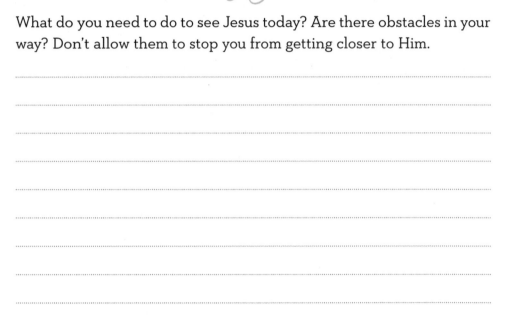

What do you need to do to see Jesus today? Are there obstacles in your way? Don't allow them to stop you from getting closer to Him.

And, behold, there was a man named Zacchaeus, which was the chief among the publicans, and he was rich. And he sought to see Jesus who he was; and could not for the press, because he was little of stature. And he ran before, and climbed up into a sycomore tree to see him: for he was to pass that way.

LUKE 19:2–4

Walking by Faith

God, one day my faith shall be sight. In this life, I am called to walk by faith. In the next, I will see that which I have believed in for all these years. Earth is for faith, and heaven is for sight. Continue to nurture in me a deep faith, one that causes me to take each step of this journey with You as my focus. I walk by faith, not by sight. Amen.

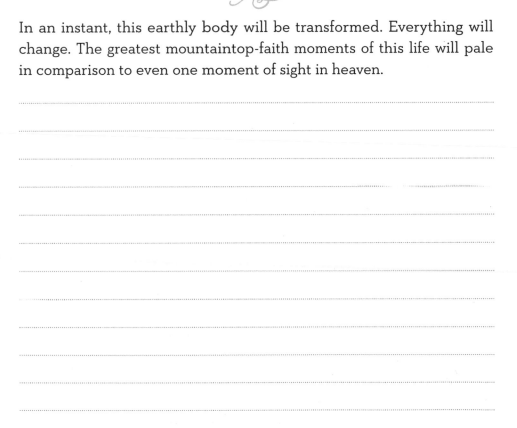

In an instant, this earthly body will be transformed. Everything will change. The greatest mountaintop-faith moments of this life will pale in comparison to even one moment of sight in heaven.

For we walk by faith, not by sight.

2 CORINTHIANS 5:7

God Cleanses the Unclean

*Father, when Peter had a vision of unclean beasts, You told him to kill
and eat, but he refused because the animals were common or unclean
in his mind. Sometimes, I've made up my mind about people before
I knew them or their story. Teach me not to judge others or the
way they live. Help me to leave that up to You. You're
able to cleanse and change them. Amen.*

Are there those you shy away from because they aren't like you? Do you
question their relationship with God? Pray for them, and leave them in
God's hands. He's the Judge.

---

*And there came a voice to him, Rise, Peter; kill, and eat. But Peter
said, Not so, Lord; for I have never eaten any thing that is common
or unclean. And the voice spake unto him again the second time,
What God hath cleansed, that call not thou common.*

ACTS 10:13–15

Resting on the Sabbath

Father, You created us as beings that work and need rest.
Sometimes I forget that. I get so caught up in all that must be
accomplished. Slow my pace, Lord. Help me to honor You by resting
one day per week. Help me to keep the Sabbath holy. Thank You
for designing the week and for telling Your people to rest.
It is up to me to follow Your command. Amen.

Do you keep the Sabbath holy? Do you conduct business? Swing by the office? Tackle that mound of laundry? Or do you set aside the whole day to honor God and to rest?

_____

_____

_____

_____

_____

_____

_____

_____

Remember the sabbath day, to keep it holy. Six days shalt thou
labour, and do all thy work: but the seventh day is the sabbath
of the LORD thy God: in it thou shalt not do any work.
EXODUS 20:8–10

Not Ashamed

Jesus, help me never to be ashamed of You or the Gospel. No matter where I am, help me to be loyal to my faith. Sometimes when I'm in a group of people who are unbelievers, I'm tempted to be silent. There are those who are very outspoken against Christianity. Give me courage so that I won't be afraid to state my belief in You. Amen.

When negative things are said about Christians, does it make you afraid or ashamed? Ask God for courage to stand in the face of those who are unbelievers. Your stand may result in the salvation of someone else.

. . . .

. . . .

. . . .

. . . .

. . . .

. . . .

. . . .

For I am not ashamed of the gospel of Christ: for it is the power of God unto salvation to every one that believeth; to the Jew first, and also to the Greek.

ROMANS 1:16

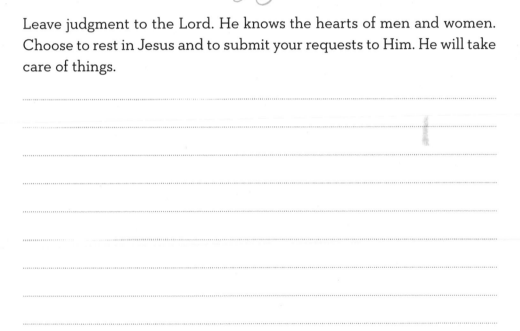

DAY 79
Rest in the Lord

Heavenly Father, take my worries and burdens. I submit to You my anxieties. Fill me with the rest that calms my spirit when I trust in You. Sometimes I look at others' lives and compare them to my own. Why do they have what I desire? Especially when I know that they are not Christians! But You tell me not to be concerned with others' prosperity. I choose to rest in You. Amen.

Leave judgment to the Lord. He knows the hearts of men and women. Choose to rest in Jesus and to submit your requests to Him. He will take care of things.

Rest in the LORD, and wait patiently for him: fret not thyself because of him who prospereth in his way, because of the man who bringeth wicked devices to pass.

PSALM 37:7

DAY 80

Where Does Your Faith Stand?

Lord, sometimes when I need advice, I turn to people around me.
I think that's okay as long as I remember that You are my main
source of help. My friends and family may support me and
encourage me, but help me to place my faith in You and
Your power to take care of every situation. Amen.

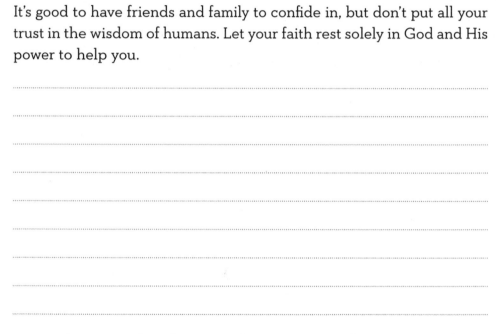

It's good to have friends and family to confide in, but don't put all your trust in the wisdom of humans. Let your faith rest solely in God and His power to help you.

_____

_____

_____

_____

_____

_____

_____

And my speech and my preaching was not with enticing words
of man's wisdom, but in demonstration of the Spirit and of
power: that your faith should not stand in the
wisdom of men, but in the power of God.

1 CORINTHIANS 2:4–5

DAY 81
Invitation to Rest

Jesus, You told Your disciples to rest. You directed them to leave the crowd and to relax and eat. You saw that they had been busy with ministry and they needed to recuperate. If You directed them to rest, even these twelve who worked at Your side daily, You must want me to rest as well. Remind me to take breaks from ministry. I needed to hear that You give me permission to rest! Amen.

Legalism says to sign up for this, that, and the other ministry. It calls you to work beyond what Jesus desires. Listen to the Lord. He invites you to rest.

And he said unto them, Come ye yourselves apart into a desert place, and rest a while: for there were many coming and going, and they had no leisure so much as to eat.

MARK 6:31

Godly Weapons

Father, sometimes the battle between right and wrong gets tedious.
The enemy tries to draw my focus away from You and toward things
that are ungodly. Help me to rely on You. I cannot fight the battle
alone. I need supernatural power to resist the thoughts and
imaginations the devil brings to my mind. Amen.

Are you trying to fight a battle all by yourself? You don't have to. God
has given us the weapon of His Spirit and power to overcome every
temptation that comes our way. Rely on Him.

(For the weapons of our warfare are not carnal, but mighty through
God to the pulling down of strong holds;) casting down imaginations,
and every high thing that exalteth itself against the knowledge of God,
and bringing into captivity every thought to the obedience of Christ.

2 CORINTHIANS 10:4–5

DAY 83

Still before the Lord

Father, as I am still before You this morning, I focus on who You are. You are sovereign, all-knowing, and You have plans to prosper and not to harm me. You are the Prince of Peace, my Provider, my Protector, and my Friend. You are holy, and yet You draw near to me when I draw near to You. You are the one true God. And I worship You in the quiet of this morning. Amen.

There is a reason that scripture says to *be still*. Our minds and bodies need to be still before Him in order to focus on who God is.

Be still, and know that I am God: I will be exalted among the heathen, I will be exalted in the earth.

PSALM 46:10

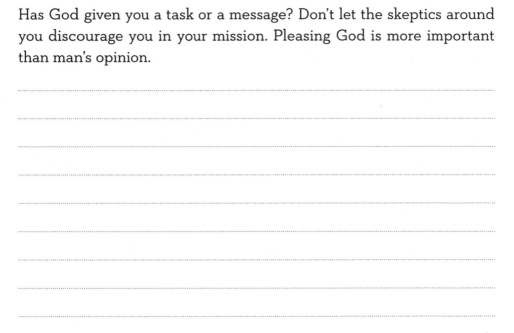

DAY 84

Pleasing God

*Father, sometimes I care too much what people think instead
of what You would have me do. Give me the courage to seek
You and Your will for my life. Let me strive to be Your servant
even in the face of criticism and what people say
I should do. Pleasing You is my goal. Amen.*

Has God given you a task or a message? Don't let the skeptics around
you discourage you in your mission. Pleasing God is more important
than man's opinion.

*As we said before, so say I now again, if any man preach any other
gospel unto you than that ye have received, let him be accursed.
For do I now persuade men, or God? or do I seek to please men?
for if I yet pleased men, I should not be the servant of Christ.*

GALATIANS 1:9–10

Calming the Storms

Lord, sometimes You calm storms, and other times You carry Your children through them. There is a storm raging in my heart. I ask that You end it, but I desire Your will for my life. If I must walk through this storm, will You go with me every step of the way? You are where my heart finds rest and peace, regardless of the outward circumstances. I love You, Lord. Amen.

Wouldn't it have been amazing to witness Jesus calming the storm from the boat that day? What storms has He calmed in your life?

_____

_____

_____

_____

_____

_____

_____

_____

_____

_____

_____

And he arose, and rebuked the wind, and said unto the sea, Peace, be still. And the wind ceased, and there was a great calm.

MARK 4:39

Walk in Light

Jesus, there are those who tell us we need to be tolerant of all people and who they are. We're encouraged to accept them no matter how they live. Your Word tells me to walk in light and not have fellowship with darkness. Show me how to be a witness to those in darkness as I attempt to walk in the light. Amen.

We cannot participate in the sinful lifestyle of those who don't know Christ, but we must let our lights shine so those in darkness can find their way out of sin and bondage also.

For ye were sometimes darkness, but now are ye light in the Lord: walk as children of light: (for the fruit of the Spirit is in all goodness and righteousness and truth;) proving what is acceptable unto the Lord. And have no fellowship with the unfruitful works of darkness, but rather reprove them.

EPHESIANS 5:8–11

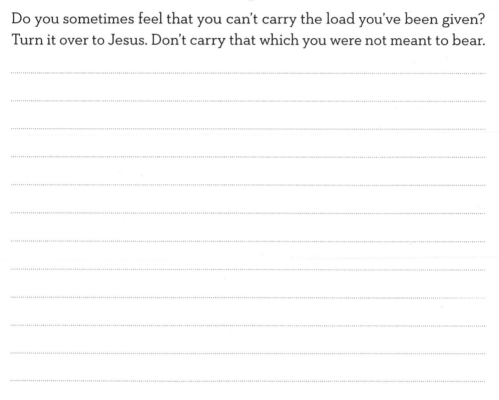

DAY 87

Come to Jesus

I come to You, Lord Jesus. That is the first step. I come before You now in this quiet moment. As I begin this new day, calm my spirit. There is work that must be done today. But even as I work, I can find rest in You. Ease the tension and stress in me, Lord, as only You can do. Thank You for a sense of peace. Amen.

Do you sometimes feel that you can't carry the load you've been given? Turn it over to Jesus. Don't carry that which you were not meant to bear.

*Come unto me, all ye that labour and
are heavy laden, and I will give you rest.*
MATTHEW 11:28

Sing unto the Lord

Lord, I bless Your name and give You thanks for Your blessings on my life. Knowing You has given me a new song to sing. My voice may not be the best, but I want to sing unto You, for You are worthy of all my praise whether it be singing or speaking. Amen.

Take time to praise the Lord today by singing a song out loud to Him. Forget about how your voice sounds; just lift it up and give Him praise.

_____

_____

_____

_____

_____

_____

_____

_____

_____

_____

_____

*O sing unto the LORD a new song: sing unto the LORD,
all the earth. Sing unto the LORD, bless his name;
shew forth his salvation from day to day.*

PSALM 96:1–2

Relaxation

Thank You, God, for the gift of relaxation. It is so nice to sit out on a patio in springtime or by the fireplace in winter and enjoy a good meal with friends or family. It is relaxing to my mind, my heart, and my spirit. Help me to always set aside time to fellowship with others and to relax. Thank You for this blessing. Amen.

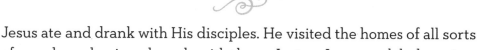

Jesus ate and drank with His disciples. He visited the homes of all sorts of people and enjoyed meals with them. Just as Jesus modeled service, He also demonstrated relaxation.

There is nothing better for a man, than that he should eat and drink, and that he should make his soul enjoy good in his labour. This also I saw, that it was from the hand of God. For who can eat, or who else can hasten hereunto, more than I?

ECCLESIASTES 2:24-25

Sow Some Seed

Jesus, I don't always see results from the seed I've sown into other people's lives. They either don't seem interested in hearing the Gospel or when they do listen, the devil comes along and entices them away. Help me not to focus on the end result but be faithful to sow seed to those around me, leaving the results to You. Amen.

When you sow Gospel seeds into other people's lives, leave the end result up to Jesus.

I have planted, Apollos watered; but God gave the increase. So then neither is he that planteth any thing, neither he that watereth; but God that giveth the increase. Now he that planteth and he that watereth are one: and every man shall receive his own reward according to his own labour.

1 CORINTHIANS 3:6–8

DAY 91
Finding Balance

Jesus, when I think of Your ministry here on earth, I picture You teaching and casting out demons. You fed the five thousand and conversed with the woman at the well. You raised Lazarus from the dead! What a flurry of activity! But then I read that You slept...and during a storm that was frightening Your friends. If You rested, so shall I. I will set aside my work when it is appropriate to rest. Amen.

Some people do nothing but work. Others are lazy. Jesus desires a balanced life for you. Work and play are both good for you. Establish balance between the two.

And, behold, there arose a great tempest in the sea, insomuch that the ship was covered with the waves: but he was asleep.

MATTHEW 8:24

One Body in Christ

Lord, sometimes I'm frustrated with the way things are in churches. I wonder why some people are given certain positions and others a lesser place. I'd like to change things sometimes, but I know it's not my place to make changes. Calm me down, Lord. Help me to remember that You have placed people in the body of Christ where You want to use them. Amen.

Do you ever wonder why God chooses to use people in the way He does? Don't fret about it. Leave it up to Him. It's His choice, not yours.

....

....

....

....

....

....

....

....

....

....

....

But now hath God set the members every one of them in the body, as it hath pleased him.
1 CORINTHIANS 12:18

Peaceful Sleep

Father, thank You for the refreshment that sleep provides. I know it is Your desire that I rest after working all day. I will not fear the darkness of the night. I have nothing to be afraid of because You watch over me. Thank You for sweet, peaceful sleep. As I go about my day today, give me energy for the tasks at hand. And when evening comes, grant me rest again, I pray. Amen.

Make the closing activity of the day a conversation with God. Talking with your heavenly Father and casting your cares on Him will help you to rest easy through the night.

....

....

....

....

....

....

....

....

....

When thou liest down, thou shalt not be afraid: yea, thou shalt lie down, and thy sleep shall be sweet.

PROVERBS 3:24

Strengthened by His Spirit

Father, Paul prayed for the Ephesians that they would be strengthened with might by Your Spirit in their inner man. I need that same strength that can only come from You. He goes on to pray that they will be rooted and grounded in love and that they would know the love of Christ and be filled with all the fullness of God. I ask that Paul's prayer take effect in my own life each day. Amen.

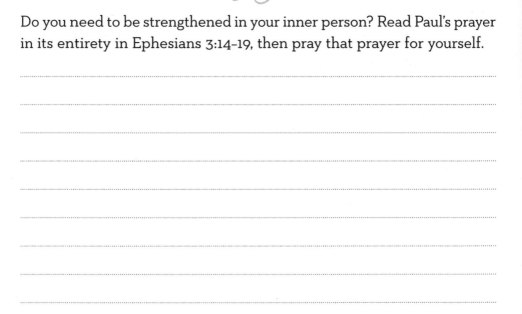

Do you need to be strengthened in your inner person? Read Paul's prayer in its entirety in Ephesians 3:14–19, then pray that prayer for yourself.

_____

_____

_____

_____

_____

_____

_____

_____

For this cause I bow my knees unto the Father of our Lord Jesus Christ, of whom the whole family in heaven and earth is named, that he would grant you, according to the riches of his glory, to be strengthened with might by his Spirit in the inner man.

EPHESIANS 3:14–16

Patience in a Busy World

Father, patience isn't easy. This is a busy, fast-paced world in which I exist! I drive through fast-food restaurant windows and receive hot food within a few minutes. Automated bank tellers provide cash in an instant. There is not much I have to wait for in this modern age. But I realize that some of the things that matter most require great patience. Teach me to wait with grace. Amen.

If you are waiting for something you desire, trust God. The Bible promises that He will not withhold any good and perfect gift from His children.

Now we exhort you, brethren, warn them that are unruly, comfort the feebleminded, support the weak, be patient toward all men.

1 THESSALONIANS 5:14

Knowing Christ

Lord, thank You for all I have attained in life. I've been blessed greatly, but no matter how successful I may become or how much I know or learn, none of it is more important than knowing You. No degree or acclaim from man can take the place of the knowledge of You and the gift of salvation You have provided. Amen.

No matter what you have attained in life, remember that knowing Christ is the only thing that counts in eternity.

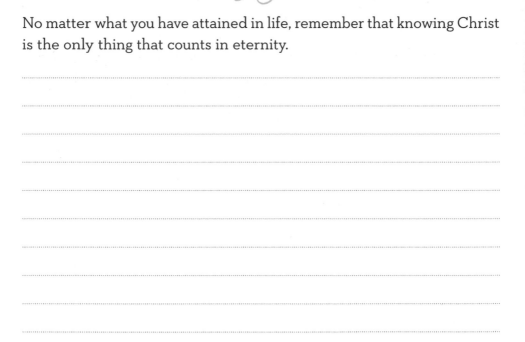

But what things were gain to me, those I counted loss for Christ. Yea doubtless, and I count all things but loss for the excellency of the knowledge of Christ Jesus my Lord: for whom I have suffered the loss of all things, and do count them but dung, that I may win Christ.

PHILIPPIANS 3:7–8

Waiting for Christ's Return

*Lord Jesus, the evening news reports are full of sadness. At times,
I wonder why You are waiting. Why don't You come back for Your
people? Why don't You take us out of this world full of sin and pain?
I know there is a better place, another life waiting for us in heaven.
Give me patience. No one knows the day that You will return.
As I wait, may I keep my eyes fixed on You. Amen.*

The media seem to focus on reporting about the negative. Try writing
in a "thankful journal" each morning as you begin your day. What are
you thankful for?

_____

_____

_____

_____

_____

_____

_____

*Be patient therefore, brethren, unto the coming of the Lord. Behold,
the husbandman waiteth for the precious fruit of the earth, and hath
long patience for it, until he receive the early and latter rain. Be ye also
patient; stablish your hearts: for the coming of the Lord draweth nigh.*

JAMES 5:7–8

Pray for Those in Authority

*Father, remember our leaders and those in charge of our country.
Give them wisdom and knowledge for every decision. Let them seek
Your will in their personal lives as well as the welfare of our country.
Protect them as they go about their duties. Amen.*

Do you pray for those in authority? The Bible encourages us to do so.
When you pray, ask God to give our leaders wisdom in making decisions
on our behalf.

_____

_____

_____

_____

_____

_____

_____

_____

*I exhort therefore, that, first of all, supplications, prayers, intercessions,
and giving of thanks, be made for all men; for kings, and for all that
are in authority; that we may lead a quiet and peaceable life in all
godliness and honesty. For this is good and acceptable in the sight
of God our Saviour; who will have all men to be saved,
and to come unto the knowledge of the truth.*

1 TIMOTHY 2:1–4

Slow to Speak

Father, I am often the opposite of what James advises in these verses. I catch myself being quick to speak and slow to listen. I make assumptions and find out later I was wrong. I say things and later wish I had gotten all the facts first. Lord, I admit that this is not an easy task—being patient with those around me. Please put a guard over my tongue. Amen.

The first step to change is admitting there is a problem. If you want to be quicker to listen and slower to speak, admit that it is tough. . .and then try to do better. God will bless your efforts.

Wherefore, my beloved brethren, let every man be swift to hear, slow to speak, slow to wrath: for the wrath of man worketh not the righteousness of God.

JAMES 1:19–20

DAY 100
Proper Priorities

Jesus, sometimes I get bogged down in the daily duties of life. I get so tangled up with the events of the day that I forget the really important things, like prayer and Bible study. It's easy at those times for the enemy to entice me away from what I know I should be doing, which is being a good soldier in Your army. Forgive me. Clear the cobwebs from my mind. Help me to remember where my priorities lie. Amen.

What are your priorities today? Are you so tangled up in the responsibilities of life that you haven't taken time to pray or read your Bible? Decide today that you will get your priorities in their proper order.

No man that warreth entangleth himself with the affairs of this life; that he may please him who hath chosen him to be a soldier.

2 TIMOTHY 2:4

Patient but Not Lazy

Jesus, there is so much work to be done. There are so many who have not heard the good news of Christ yet! As Your people, we must be about kingdom work and spreading the Gospel. You have given us the great commission to go into the world and tell others. But we must also be patient in our faith as we await the perfect timing of Your second coming! Amen.

There is a time for everything. In Ecclesiastes, we are told that there is a time to work and a time to rest. Be patient but not lazy.

That ye be not slothful, but followers of them who through faith and patience inherit the promises.

HEBREWS 6:12

Words Fitly Spoken

*Father, sometimes my words aren't what the Bible calls "fitly spoken."
I have a habit of speaking without thinking on occasion. I really don't
want to do that, but the human side of me gets in the way of my
trying to become more like You. Help me to think before I speak,
and let my words glorify You and encourage others. Amen.*

Our words give us away sometimes. We try to put our best foot forward,
and then we stick that same foot in our mouths and out come the wrong
words. Ask God to help you speak the right words at the right time.

_____

_____

_____

_____

_____

_____

_____

_____

_____

_____

A word fitly spoken is like apples of gold in pictures of silver.
PROVERBS 25:11

Patience with Others

Father, make me a little more like Jesus each day. Make me sensitive to the Holy Spirit when I am tempted to be impatient. Let me be known as one who is kind, merciful, and humble. When others describe me, I am not sure they would use these adjectives. Just as You bear with me, help me to bear with my family, friends, and colleagues with a spirit of forgiveness. Amen.

God has forgiven you. Forgive others. God has been patient with you. Be patient with others.

Put on therefore, as the elect of God, holy and beloved, bowels of mercies, kindness, humbleness of mind, meekness, longsuffering; forbearing one another, and forgiving one another, if any man have a quarrel against any: even as Christ forgave you, so also do ye.
COLOSSIANS 3:12–13

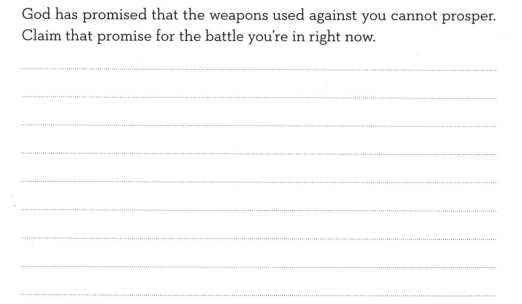

DAY 104

Victory Is Our Heritage

*Jesus, I feel like the enemy is getting the upper hand sometimes.
He throws one obstacle after the other in my path and I stumble right
over them. Your Word tells me that no weapon formed against me shall
prosper. Open my eyes so I can see the path in front of me, and give
me victory over the weapons the enemy hurls at me. Amen.*

God has promised that the weapons used against you cannot prosper.
Claim that promise for the battle you're in right now.

_____

_____

_____

_____

_____

_____

_____

_____

*No weapon that is formed against thee shall prosper; and every
tongue that shall rise against thee in judgment thou shalt
condemn. This is the heritage of the servants of the LORD,
and their righteousness is of me, saith the LORD.*

Isaiah 54:17

Slow to Anger

Lord, like a virus, a spirit of dissatisfaction spreads quickly. It can infect everyone who comes near. You warn me in Your Word about this. You want Your people to be slow to anger. Help me to be aware of the impact my attitude and my reactions have on those within my sphere of influence. I truly want to be a peacemaker and not one who is known for stirring up trouble. Amen.

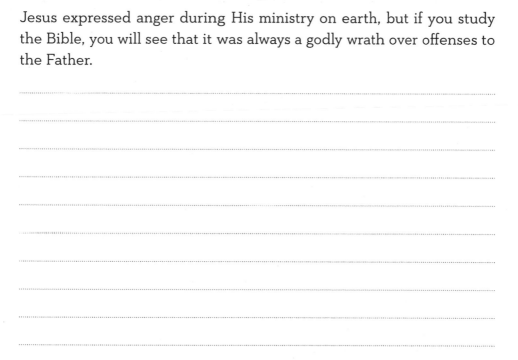

Jesus expressed anger during His ministry on earth, but if you study the Bible, you will see that it was always a godly wrath over offenses to the Father.

*A wrathful man stirreth up strife:
but he that is slow to anger appeaseth strife.*

PROVERBS 15:18

Thirsty for God

Father, I'm thirsty for more of You. Without Your touch, I wander around in the desert of my life, parched and lost. Draw me close to You; refresh my dry and thirsty spirit. You have an endless well of life-giving water, and I need a drink from that well. Help me to draw deeply from Your resources. Amen.

You don't have to wander around thirsty. God has a well of spiritual water to draw from. Lower your bucket into His well.

O God, thou art my God; early will I seek thee: my soul thirsteth for thee, my flesh longeth for thee in a dry and thirsty land, where no water is; to see thy power and thy glory, so as I have seen thee in the sanctuary.

PSALM 63:1–2

Following Christ's Example

*Lord, You are always there, and You are consistently patient with me.
What if it were not so? What if You reached Your limit and showed the
wrath that I deserve in my sinful imperfection? Because of Your great
patience with me, let me not grow tired of being patient myself.
Let me model what You have shown me by Your example.
Thank You for Your great patience with me, God. Amen.*

Anything that Jesus asks of us He models well. Get to know the Savior
through prayer and the reading of His Word, and His character traits
will become apparent in you.

*And let us not be weary in well doing:
for in due season we shall reap, if we faint not.*

GALATIANS 6:9

Stand Strong

Jesus, some days I don't understand the obstacles I face. It seems that when I'm trying my best, working my hardest, I run into all kinds of problems. The human side of me asks why. I know that the devil is out to destroy anything done for Your glory. Give me strength to accomplish the task You have set for me to do. Help me to focus on You and not the obstacles. Amen.

When God has a job for us to do, Satan will try to interfere. Press on. Don't give up. Jesus said He overcame the world, and we can too.

And he shall be like a tree planted by the rivers of water, that bringeth forth his fruit in his season; his leaf also shall not wither; and whatsoever he doeth shall prosper.

PSALM 1:3

Renewing My Strength

Heavenly Father, I am amazed by all the energy drinks and power bars available these days at the grocery store. If only everyone could see that true strength, true energy comes from You! Certainly exercise and good nutrition are helpful. But inner strength, the type that endures life's hardships and trials, is found only in a relationship with Christ. I am so thankful I have this great source of strength. Amen.

Patience develops perseverance. If you want to finish the race well, learn to wait patiently upon the Lord.

But they that wait upon the LORD shall renew their strength; they shall mount up with wings as eagles; they shall run, and not be weary; and they shall walk, and not faint.

ISAIAH 40:31

The Glory of God

*Father, every time I look at the stars or see the sun shining,
I'm reminded of Your greatness. They speak to Your power and
majesty; they remain in the heavens consistently doing their job.
Even when it's storming, somewhere the sun or the stars are shining,
giving out their light. Lord, enable me to do the same. Help me to shine
for You no matter what kind of storm is brewing in my life. Amen.*

The children of God can shine for Him even when they're facing a storm.
Don't let the clouds put out your light.

*The heavens declare the glory of God;
and the firmament sheweth his handywork.*

PSALM 19:1

Patience and Wisdom

Father, patience and wisdom seem to go hand in hand. I am beginning to determine that the wisest people I know are also some of the most patient. They seek You in every trial. They exhibit Your character traits. Give me patience. Help me to be still before You and to seek You in my life. May I grow in wisdom through being patient as You teach and stretch me. Amen.

If you want to be wise, read God's Word. Take your time with it. Ask God to instruct you and change you through His Word. Patience is a key to wisdom.

But the wisdom that is from above is first pure, then peaceable, gentle, and easy to be intreated, full of mercy and good fruits, without partiality, and without hypocrisy.

JAMES 3:17

A High Priest

Jesus, I hate to see others suffering in pain. I feel so helpless. I can't take away their pain. I'm so glad I know You and have the privilege of praying and asking You for help. You have experienced great pain and suffered beyond my comprehension. You are touched by the feelings we have and show great compassion for Your children. Thank You. Amen.

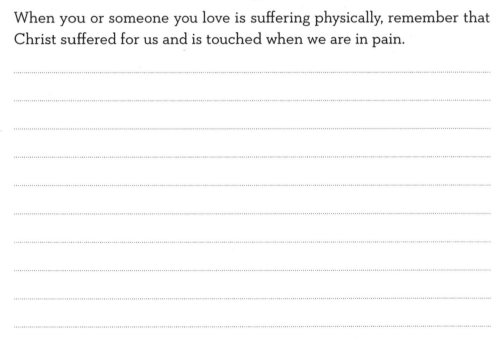

When you or someone you love is suffering physically, remember that Christ suffered for us and is touched when we are in pain.

....

....

....

....

....

....

....

....

For we have not an high priest which cannot be touched with the feeling of our infirmities; but was in all points tempted like as we are, yet without sin.

HEBREWS 4:15

DAY 113
In Christ's Strength

*Father, I am so thankful for the strength that is mine as a Christian.
I cannot do anything on my own, but through Christ, I can do all
things. It is comforting to know that the word all includes the trials and
concerns that I bring to You this morning. I lay them at
Your feet, Lord. I take You at Your Word. I can do all
things through Jesus who lives in me. Amen.*

Recognizing that it is Christ who strengthens you takes some of the pressure off. You can't do it on your own. Focus instead on your strength through Him!

I can do all things through Christ which strengtheneth me.
Philippians 4:13

Come Boldly to the Throne

Jesus, thank You for the work on the cross. Because of Your sacrifice, I have entrance into the holy of holies—the throne room of God. I can go directly to the Father and make my requests known unto Him. And You're right there with Him, making intercession on my behalf. I don't have to be afraid; I can come boldly to the throne because of You and Your sacrifice. Amen.

When you have a problem, you don't have to make an appointment to see a specialist; you can go directly to the throne of God and speak with Him personally.

Let us therefore come boldly unto the throne of grace, that we may obtain mercy, and find grace to help in time of need.

HEBREWS 4:16

Strength to Combat Temptation

*God, at times I sink so deep into temptation that I forget Your promise.
You have said that there is always a way out, a way of escape.
You have promised in Your Word that nothing is strong enough
to separate me from Your love. I confess to You this morning that
temptation is alive and well in my heart. Set my eyes on the
way of escape. Free me from temptation, I pray. Amen.*

Whatever the temptation that pulls at your heartstrings, Jesus is stronger.
Jesus is for you and never against you. He has provided an exit sign.
Flee temptation to sin.

_____

_____

_____

_____

_____

_____

_____

_____

*There hath no temptation taken you but such as is common to man:
but God is faithful, who will not suffer you to be tempted above
that ye are able; but will with the temptation also make
a way to escape, that ye may be able to bear it.*

1 CORINTHIANS 10:13

Lay Aside the Weight

Lord, I'm so thankful for those who have gone before us to pave the way. They looked for the promise of a Messiah. You came and made a way for us. Give me strength to press on and run the race with patience. Help me to lay aside everything that would hinder me and keep me from making it to the end. Amen.

Nothing is more important than finishing the race to heaven.

Wherefore seeing we also are compassed about with so great a cloud of witnesses, let us lay aside every weight, and the sin which doth so easily beset us, and let us run with patience the race that is set before us, looking unto Jesus the author and finisher of our faith; who for the joy that was set before him endured the cross, despising the shame, and is set down at the right hand of the throne of God.

HEBREWS 12:1–2

My Source of Strength

*Father, at times I worry too much about what others think of me.
Even when I just have a minor disagreement with a friend or coworker,
I am afraid that the person will not like me anymore. I worry that
I have not lived up to what was expected of me. Remind me,
Father, that I must seek my ultimate strength and
encouragement from You and You alone. Amen.*

Remember that your position before God has been established through Christ. It is secure. God sees you as His precious daughter. Find strength in this.

*And David was greatly distressed; for the people spake of
stoning him, because the soul of all the people was grieved,
every man for his sons and for his daughters: but David
encouraged himself in the LORD his God.*

1 SAMUEL 30:6

A Ready Answer

*Lord, thank You for salvation and Your ever-present Spirit in my life.
I want to share this wonderful experience with others. Give me wisdom
and knowledge and a ready answer when someone asks me about You
and my faith. Give me courage to share the reason for my hope and to
invite others to experience Your love and gift of salvation. Amen.*

Word of mouth is a great way to share experiences with others. Be ready
to share Christ with everyone who asks you about your faith.

*But sanctify the Lord God in your hearts: and be ready always
to give an answer to every man that asketh you a reason
of the hope that is in you with meekness and fear.*

1 PETER 3:15

God Is with Me

Heavenly Father, as I meet with You this morning, I find great strength in the knowledge that You will never leave me. Wherever I go, You are there with me. You are not just beside me, but You reside in my heart. I never have to be afraid. The Lord Almighty, the Maker of heaven and earth, is with me. Thank You, Father, for the strength I find in You. Amen.

When life throws you a curveball and you are confused, remember that God is still with you. He will never leave you or forsake you.

Have not I commanded thee? Be strong and of a good courage; be not afraid, neither be thou dismayed: for the LORD thy God is with thee whithersoever thou goest.

JOSHUA 1:9

Don't Be Ashamed

Jesus, sometimes when I'm surrounded by unbelievers speaking harsh words about Christians, I'm tempted to remain silent because of fear. But You spoke up even when it meant Your life was at stake. I never want to be ashamed of the Gospel. Give me boldness through the Holy Spirit to stand for You at all costs. Amen.

Does fear show itself when you're confronted about your faith? Ask God for boldness to stand up for Jesus.

O my God, I trust in thee: let me not be ashamed, let not mine enemies triumph over me.

PSALM 25:2

Mountain-Moving Faith

I cannot imagine, Jesus, that anything I could do would compare to Your works. But You taught, when You were here on earth, that there is great strength in faith. On more than one occasion You told Your followers that they could do greater things even than You had done. The source? Faith. Give me that type of faith, Lord. The type of faith that moves mountains! Amen.

Some days it may seem that your faith is small. Jesus said that there is great power even in faith the size of a tiny mustard seed.

Jesus answered and said unto them, Verily I say unto you, If ye have faith, and doubt not, ye shall not only do this which is done to the fig tree, but also if ye shall say unto this mountain, Be thou removed, and be thou cast into the sea; it shall be done.

MATTHEW 21:21

Be Vigilant

*Father, I know the devil is trying to work overtime on many Christians.
He's looking for someone to devour. Give me boldness to live for You.
Make me sober and vigilant, always watching for his traps. Help me
to resist him in faith, claiming Your promises of victory.
Give me wisdom to know every direction I should
take, every decision I should make. Amen.*

Be on your guard. Don't allow Satan to trip you up. Be steadfast in your
faith, and resist him by your faith in God.

---

*Be sober, be vigilant; because your adversary the devil,
as a roaring lion, walketh about, seeking whom he may devour:
whom resist stedfast in the faith, knowing that the same afflictions
are accomplished in your brethren that are in the world.*

1 PETER 5:8–9

Fear No Evil

*How wonderful, God, that death has no power over the Christian!
You are a strong and mighty God, the one true God. You are with
me, protecting me all the way. And when the end of this life comes,
whenever that may be, You will walk with me through the valley
of the shadow of death. Death has lost its sting because
Christ has conquered it! In Your name, I pray, amen.*

There is great strength for the believer in Christ who faces even a terminal illness. We will all die a physical death, but our spirits will live for eternity with Jesus!

*Yea, though I walk through the valley of the shadow of death, I will fear
no evil: for thou art with me; thy rod and thy staff they comfort me.*

PSALM 23:4

God Knows Our Needs

Father, You are so good to Your children. You know all about my needs and sometimes You meet those needs without me asking. Unexpected blessings that come my way lift my heart and give me reason to praise You. I'm so glad to serve a God like You who is aware of what I need even before I ask You. Amen.

Trust God to meet your needs. He already knows what they are. Sometimes He's just waiting for us to ask. At other times, He sends an answer before we pray.

Be not ye therefore like unto them: for your Father knoweth what things ye have need of, before ye ask him.
MATTHEW 6:8

A Spirit of Power

God, a spirit of fear is not from You! It is from the enemy. I choose to believe the promise from Your Word that You have given believers a spirit of power, love, and a sound mind. I will go about my day with strength. I will love others well. I will make solid and right decisions based on Your living Word. I claim this promise. You are my strength! Amen.

Messages that whisper what you *cannot* do are from the evil one. God's messages for you will always be concerning what you *can* do. Through Christ, you are able.

For God hath not given us the spirit of fear; but of power, and of love, and of a sound mind.

2 TIMOTHY 1:7

Do Good to All

Jesus, You've told us to do unto others what we want others to do unto us. Sometimes that is so hard because what people do to me sometimes is mean, painful, and ugly. When I'm hurting because of their actions, my first impulse is to defend myself, and that means saying something that might hurt them. Forgive me, and help me to remember Your words and to treat others in the same way I want to be treated. I know that's what pleases You. Amen.

Whenever people mistreat you, remember the words of Jesus and treat them in the way you wish they had treated you. Pleasing God with our actions is more important than getting revenge.

Therefore all things whatsoever ye would that men should do to you, do ye even so to them: for this is the law and the prophets.

MATTHEW 7:12

DAY 127
My Strength and My Song

Lord, You don't just provide my strength. You ARE my strength.
Through You, I am able to do all things. At times I forget this. I lean on
my own strength, which is never enough. It always fails me. Today I will
stand firm on my foundation, which is salvation through Christ.
I will find my strength in the one true God. I will
worship You with my life. Amen.

When unbelievers ask you how you are so strong when facing tough circumstances, always give the glory to God. He is glorified when you give Him credit for your strength.

....

....

....

....

....

....

....

The LORD is my strength and song, and he is become my salvation:
he is my God, and I will prepare him an habitation;
my father's God, and I will exalt him.
EXODUS 15:2

None of These Things Move Me

Lord, the apostle Paul suffered many things at the hands of cruel people, but he said that none of these things moved him or pulled him away from You. He was determined to finish the race. He wasn't going to give up because he was suffering. Lord, give me that same determination to finish the race no matter what. Help me to say along with Paul, "None of these things move me." Amen.

When you face trials and temptations, keep your mind focused on finishing the race. Don't let any of those things move you away from your relationship with God.

_____

_____

_____

_____

_____

_____

_____

_____

But none of these things move me, neither count I my life dear unto myself, so that I might finish my course with joy, and the ministry, which I have received of the Lord Jesus, to testify the gospel of the grace of God.

ACTS 20:24

Sharing the Good News

*Why do I find it so hard just to open my mouth and share the Gospel?
Give me strength, Lord, to share the good news of Jesus with others.
When the opportunity presents itself, even today, I ask that You will
give me strength to share openly. The world needs You. I have
received the Good News, and it is my responsibility to spread
the word. Empower me, I pray. In Your name, amen.*

The strength for sharing the Gospel with another must come directly
from Christ. At the very same time, the Holy Spirit must miraculously
draw the new believer unto Himself.

....

....

....

....

....

....

....

....

*Notwithstanding the Lord stood with me, and strengthened me; that by
me the preaching might be fully known, and that all the Gentiles might
hear: and I was delivered out of the mouth of the lion.*

2 TIMOTHY 4:17

Examine Me, Lord

Lord, I'm trying to walk in Your ways. I make mistakes, but I want to remain faithful. I don't want anything in my life that will hinder me from walking with You. Examine me, Lord, and see if I need to repent. Even when I'm tried, let me remain firm in my commitment to You. Amen.

Are you afraid to ask the Lord to examine your life? It's for your benefit that He examines you and shows you where to improve.

Judge me, O Lord; for I have walked in mine integrity: I have trusted also in the Lord; therefore I shall not slide. Examine me, O Lord, and prove me; try my reins and my heart.

Psalm 26:1–2

He Is Strong

God, please show Yourself strong in my time of need! I need Your strength today. Just as the song says, "I am weak, but You are strong." I am so thankful for that exception today. "But You are strong." I will cling to that. When I am at my very weakest, when there seems to be no way I can face the future, I will face it in Your strength. Show Yourself strong in my life. In Jesus' name, amen.

"Jesus loves me. This I know, for the Bible tells me so. Little ones to Him belong. They are weak, *but He is strong.*"

_____

_____

_____

_____

_____

_____

_____

_____

For the eyes of the LORD run to and fro throughout the whole earth, to shew himself strong in the behalf of them whose heart is perfect toward him.

2 CHRONICLES 16:9

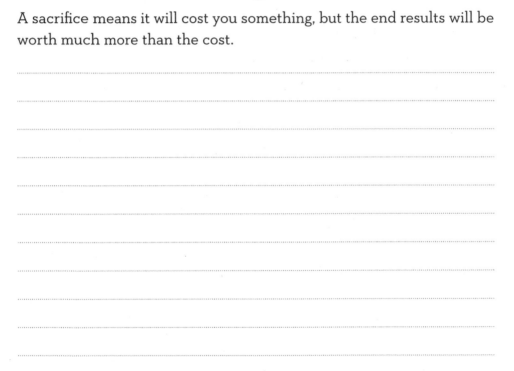

DAY 132

A Living Sacrifice

Father, Your Word says I need to present my body a living sacrifice.
A sacrifice that is holy and acceptable unto You. That means I need to
give up anything that isn't pure or clean. Father, I confess my sins
and ask You to show me how to live an acceptable, holy life.
Help me to be willing to sacrifice my will for Yours. Amen.

A sacrifice means it will cost you something, but the end results will be worth much more than the cost.

I beseech you therefore, brethren, by the mercies of God,
that ye present your bodies a living sacrifice, holy,
acceptable unto God, which is your reasonable service.

ROMANS 12:1

DAY 133

He Increases My Strength

All I have ever known is this body, Father. All I know is becoming weary. This body grows weak at times. But You are different. You never grow tired. You don't sleep or look away. Your eye is always upon my life. Your strength is consistent and eternal. Renew my strength, Lord. I need physical and spiritual power to live in this world. Thank You for strengthening me! Amen.

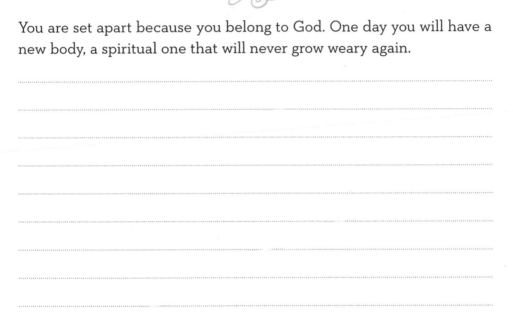

You are set apart because you belong to God. One day you will have a new body, a spiritual one that will never grow weary again.

He giveth power to the faint; and to them that have no might he increaseth strength. Even the youths shall faint and be weary, and the young men shall utterly fall: but they that wait upon the LORD shall renew their strength; they shall mount up with wings as eagles; they shall run, and not be weary; and they shall walk, and not faint.

ISAIAH 40:29–31

Given to Hospitality

Lord, there are days when I just want to be by myself. I don't want anyone else around. Forgive me. Your Word encourages us to be given to hospitality. If I'm to be more like You, I need to open my heart and my home to those who may need a friend or a visit. Fill me with more of Your love, and give me a heart that is given to hospitality. Amen.

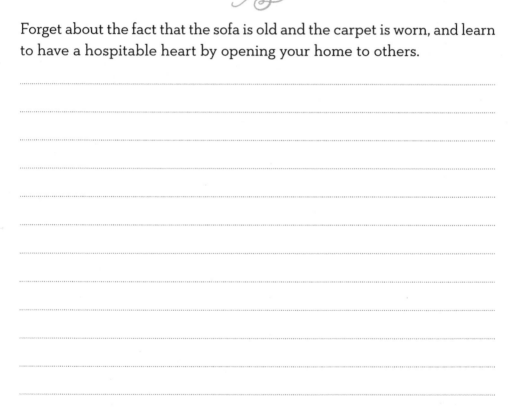

Forget about the fact that the sofa is old and the carpet is worn, and learn to have a hospitable heart by opening your home to others.

Rejoicing in hope; patient in tribulation; continuing instant in prayer; distributing to the necessity of saints; given to hospitality.

ROMANS 12:12–13

Influencing Children

Lord, let Your Word and Your ways season my conversations. I am to be salt and light in the world. May I truly be such for those that look up to me. I know there is great power in influence. Attitudes and opinions are easily noted by children, who may be young but are quick to pick up on adults' feelings. I pray that the subtleties in my conversations and actions will honor You. Amen.

Whether or not you are a mother, you influence the children in your life. Children need to see Jesus in you.

_____

_____

_____

_____

_____

_____

_____

_____

And these words, which I command thee this day, shall be in thine heart: and thou shalt teach them diligently unto thy children, and shalt talk of them when thou sittest in thine house, and when thou walkest by the way, and when thou liest down, and when thou risest up.

DEUTERONOMY 6:6–7

The Temple of God

Father, let me live in a way that glorifies You. If I am the temple of God, my life needs to be a place where You are worshipped and given first priority in all I do. Sanctify me by Your power to be a dwelling place fit for the Spirit of God to dwell in. In myself, I'm not a fit temple for You, but the blood of Jesus cleanses me from all sin, making me clean. Amen.

God wants to dwell within us, but we need to be pure and sanctified from worldly influences.

_____

_____

_____

_____

_____

_____

_____

_____

_____

_____

*Know ye not that ye are the temple of God,
and that the Spirit of God dwelleth in you?*
1 CORINTHIANS 3:16

DAY 137

Starting Where I Am

*Jesus, You give tall orders! How can I teach all nations and baptize
people? Oh. . .You mean I might not even have to leave my community?
There are people all around me who don't know You, Lord. Help me
to start with those in my sphere of influence. The grocery store clerk
who seems tired and distraught. . . The teacher at my child's school
who is so lost. . . Give me the courage to reach out. Amen.*

Certainly the Lord calls us to the ends of the earth, but He is just as
concerned with the soul of your neighbor. Start where you are.

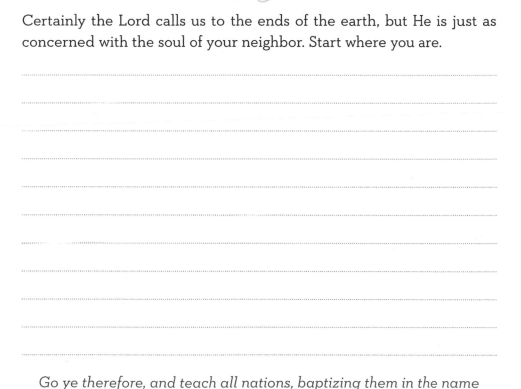

*Go ye therefore, and teach all nations, baptizing them in the name
of the Father, and of the Son, and of the Holy Ghost.*

MATTHEW 28:19

DAY 138

Alive in Christ

*Jesus, without You I would be dead in my sins. Adam's fall brought
sin into the world, but You came to bring life. People everywhere have
a wonderful opportunity to receive life because of Your sacrifice on
Calvary. I'm so glad I've been made alive through You. Thank You
for the resurrection, which means that because
You live, I can live also. Amen.*

Are you alive in Christ today? He brings life to all who receive Him. His
resurrection assures us that He is alive to give us hope.

_____

_____

_____

_____

_____

_____

_____

_____

_____

_____

_____

*For since by man came death, by man came also the resurrection of the
dead. For as in Adam all die, even so in Christ shall all be made alive.*

1 CORINTHIANS 15:21–22

Unhealthy Influences

God, please help me to know how to balance being in the world but not of it. You have blessed me with other believers to walk through life with and to receive counsel from when needed. I want to stay true to Your Word in how I live my life. I want my habits to reflect my faith. Please keep me from the power of influences that are not healthy for me. Amen.

A bad habit does not start overnight. Often, it is a series of temptations or events that pull one into it. Be on guard against such influences.

_____

_____

_____

_____

_____

_____

_____

_____

_____

Be not deceived: evil communications corrupt good manners.

1 CORINTHIANS 15:33

Blessed of the Lord

Lord, I'm so blessed to know You and to be redeemed by Your precious blood. You have forgiven my sin and made me a new person. I didn't deserve it, but You died for me and imputed Your righteousness to me because I had none of my own. You extended mercy to me when I needed it most. I'm truly blessed to be a daughter of the King. Amen.

Jesus extends to each of us exactly what we need. What are you in need of today? Forgiveness? Mercy? Grace? It's available through God's amazing love for us.

....
....
....
....
....
....
....
....
....
....
....
....
....

Blessed is he whose transgression is forgiven, whose sin is covered.

PSALM 32:1

DAY 141

Integrity

Heavenly Father, I have heard it said that integrity is doing the right thing when no one is watching. Make me aware of integrity today. When I am tempted to exceed the speed limit because I don't see a police officer. . . When the cashier forgets to scan one of the more expensive items in my cart. . . Lord, I want to be a woman of character. Help me, I pray. Amen.

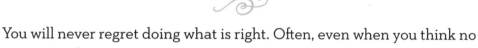

You will never regret doing what is right. Often, even when you think no one is watching, someone is.

Let integrity and uprightness preserve me; for I wait on thee.

PSALM 25:21

A New Creature

*Jesus, because of You, I'm a new person. I'm not the same
person I was in the past. All those things I lived for have lost their
importance. The sin I took pleasure in is no longer attractive
to me. You've removed all the old desires and replaced them
with new ones. Now my life is centered on You and living
a life that's pleasing to You. Thank You for new life. Amen.*

New life only comes through knowing Jesus Christ. He changes us from
the person we used to be into someone with a new purpose, new desires,
and new life.

*Therefore if any man be in Christ, he is a new creature:
old things are passed away; behold, all things are become new.*
2 CORINTHIANS 5:17

Influencing Family Members

Lord, sometimes I am discouraged because certain family members don't seem interested in spiritual matters. They are living for the world and for the moment. I long for my immediate and extended family to know Jesus as their personal Savior. Give me the words to say when the time is right. Help me to remember that the way I live is a testimony before the lost as to how great You are. Amen.

The way you handle crisis or disappointment will be watched by those who don't know Christ. They will notice the underlying peace you have, and they just may want it for themselves.

For the unbelieving husband is sanctified by the wife, and the unbelieving wife is sanctified by the husband: else were your children unclean; but now are they holy.

1 CORINTHIANS 7:14

A Willing Mind

God, I'm so glad that You accept me and my resources, and You work through them for Your glory. I don't have money, a long line of degrees, or a high position in the world, yet You are willing to use me. Thank You for the privilege of working for You. Use me and what You have blessed me with to bring glory to Your name. Amen.

God can use whatever we have if we turn it over to Him. All it takes is a willing mind on our part.

For if there be first a willing mind, it is accepted according to that a man hath, and not according to that he hath not.

2 CORINTHIANS 8:12

DAY 145

Influenced by Scripture

God, Your Word is such a gift. Often, I get so busy that I neglect my reading of it. As I open Your Word this morning, use scripture to influence my actions and reactions throughout this day. As I reflect on where I invest most of my time, help me to choose a time and place to read Your Word each day. What could be more important? Thank You for Your holy Word. Amen.

God loves you so much that He has given you a guidebook for life. It is called the Bible. It is full of His great promises and also some warnings that Christians should heed.

And that from a child thou hast known the holy scriptures, which are able to make thee wise unto salvation through faith which is in Christ Jesus. All scripture is given by inspiration of God, and is profitable for doctrine, for reproof, for correction, for instruction in righteousness.

2 TIMOTHY 3:15–16

Walk in the Spirit

Lord, help me to walk in the Spirit. When the flesh gets in my way and I give in to it, I'm ashamed because I've failed You. Without the Spirit to empower me, the flesh wants to take over. I want to live in the Spirit and walk in His presence every day that I might be an overcomer, that my life will be pleasing to You and the flesh will be defeated. Amen.

There's a constant battle between the flesh and the Spirit. The one you give in to is the one who controls you.

_____

_____

_____

_____

_____

_____

_____

_____

_____

_____

And they that are Christ's have crucified the flesh with the affections and lusts. If we live in the Spirit, let us also walk in the Spirit.

Galatians 5:24–25

DAY 147

Reflecting God's Love to Others

*Lord, I truly want to influence my little corner of the world for Christ.
Sometimes I can relate to the persecution that the heroes of the Bible
experienced. It stings when someone sarcastically says, "Pray for me!"
Help me to remember that I should never be ashamed of my faith.
Give me a kind spirit and a gentleness that reflects Your
love, regardless of the circumstances. Amen.*

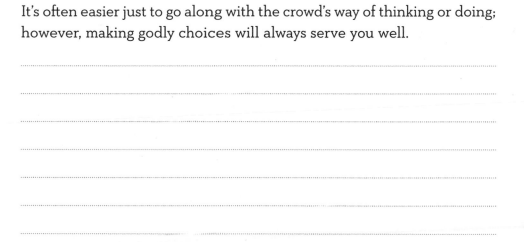

It's often easier just to go along with the crowd's way of thinking or doing;
however, making godly choices will always serve you well.

_____

_____

_____

_____

_____

_____

_____

_____

_____

*Having a good conscience; that, whereas they speak evil of you,
as of evildoers, they may be ashamed that falsely
accuse your good conversation in Christ.*

1 Peter 3:16

DAY 148

Strengthened by the Spirit

Father, Paul prayed that the Ephesian church would be strengthened by Your Spirit in their inner man so they would be rooted and grounded in love. I desire that same thing in my own life. Strengthen me, Father, by Your Spirit in my inner woman. I want to be rooted and grounded in love by Your might so others can see Christ in me. Amen.

God can strengthen you in your inner woman by His Spirit so you can be rooted and grounded in His love and become the woman He wants you to be.

That he would grant you, according to the riches of his glory, to be strengthened with might by his Spirit in the inner man.

Ephesians 3:16

Protection from Temptation

There is temptation all around me, Father. It is easy for me to say no to some of it. But there are subtle ways that Satan tempts me also. The movie that isn't appropriate. . .but all my friends are going to see. The newest style that is cute and fun. . .but a bit provocative for a Christian woman. Lord, keep my heart focused on You. Protect my heart from the influences of this world. Amen.

The writer of Proverbs got it right on this one. Don't play with fire, or you will get burned! Beware: Many of Satan's temptations in our lives are subtle.

Can a man take fire in his bosom, and his clothes not be burned?
PROVERBS 6:27

Magnify the Lord

Lord, there is a praise on my lips today. You put it there because of Your love for me. Thank You, Lord, for hearing my cry and lifting me out of the pit I was in. I praise Your name today, for You are mighty in my life. Whenever life gets tough and I forget, as humans sometimes do, let me remember to praise You anyway no matter what the situation is. Amen.

When life gets tough, praise the Lord anyway. Let there be a praise on your lips continually.

I will bless the LORD at all times: his praise shall continually be in my mouth. . . . O magnify the LORD with me, and let us exalt his name together.

PSALM 34:1, 3

Christian Friends

Thank You, Lord, for Christian friends. They help me to stay true to You. They point me back to You when I stray. As I watch the way they face problems and hear them tell of Your steadfastness in their lives, I am encouraged. There is nothing like a sister in the Lord who comes alongside and says, "Let's do life together." Thank You, Father, for my believing friends' influence in my life. Amen.

As Christians, we are in the world but not of it. Certainly, reach out to those who don't know Jesus! But those who speak into your life should walk with Christ.

He that walketh with wise men shall be wise: but a companion of fools shall be destroyed.

PROVERBS 13:20

Sing to the Lord

Lord, You've given me a song in my heart. I don't ever want to lose it. On those days, when life overwhelms me, help me to speak to myself in psalms and hymns and spiritual songs. Help me to sing a praise to You whether I feel like it or not. I've found that singing helps lift my spirit. I have much to be thankful for. Let me express my thanks in a song. Amen.

When things get tough, try singing a song of praise aloud. The devil doesn't like it when we praise God. He won't hang around too long if we're praising God for His goodness.

Speaking to yourselves in psalms and hymns and spiritual songs, singing and making melody in your heart to the Lord; giving thanks always for all things unto God and the Father in the name of our Lord Jesus Christ.

Ephesians 5:19–20

Serious Warning

Everywhere I look, Father, my society says it's okay. Sex before marriage and outside of marriage. You warn us that this type of sin is of a serious nature. What we do with our bodies stays in our hearts and minds for a very long time. Protect me from the influences in my life that say these things are permissible when Your Word clearly states they are not good for me. Amen.

The Bible does not just tell men and women to avoid fornication. It says to *flee* it! This is a serious warning from a serious God.

Flee fornication. Every sin that a man doeth is without the body; but he that committeth fornication sinneth against his own body.

1 CORINTHIANS 6:18

DAY 154

Love Not the World

Father, there are so many things in the world to entice us. If I'm not careful, I can get caught up in all the exciting, new things that come along. Show me how to enjoy what I have and not love the world. You've blessed us with so much, but help me not to put too much emphasis on material possessions. Give me a greater love for You and Your will rather than my own desires. Amen.

Be thankful for all the extras you have, but be careful that they don't take first place in your life. That position belongs to God.

Love not the world, neither the things that are in the world. If any man love the world, the love of the Father is not in him.

1 John 2:15

What Comes before God?

*Graven images? Idols? Other gods? I don't struggle with this, Lord!
You are my God! But on second thought. . .I do. My idols don't look like
those of the Old Testament. But I have them. How do I spend my time?
My money? What could be taken from me that would devastate me?
Not even a relationship or my own children should come before You.
And certainly not shopping or the latest gadgets. Amen.*

What consumes most of your time and attention? Don't let anything
come between you and the Lord. He wants to be number one in your life.

_____

_____

_____

_____

_____

_____

_____

_____

*Thou shalt not bow down thyself to them, nor serve them:
for I the LORD thy God am a jealous God, visiting the iniquity
of the fathers upon the children unto the third and
fourth generation of them that hate me.*

EXODUS 20:5

Bless Me Indeed

God, Jabez asked You to bless him and enlarge his coast. He wanted Your hand on his life. I want to pray this same prayer. I want to be blessed by You and kept from evil. Enlarge my coast in whatever ways please You. Keep Your hand on me that I might be the woman You want me to be. Bless me indeed, Lord. Amen.

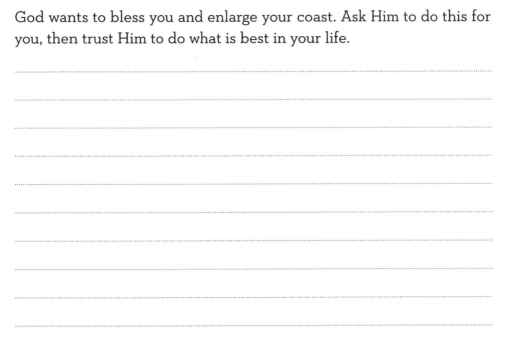

God wants to bless you and enlarge your coast. Ask Him to do this for you, then trust Him to do what is best in your life.

And Jabez called on the God of Israel, saying, Oh that thou wouldest bless me indeed, and enlarge my coast, and that thine hand might be with me, and that thou wouldest keep me from evil, that it may not grieve me! And God granted him that which he requested.

1 CHRONICLES 4:10

Confidence in the Lord

Lord, I admit it. Sometimes I am afraid. I feel helpless. My mind runs wild with anxiety. Thank You for the promise that through Christ, this is not my norm. Certainly at times, in my humanity, I cower before an unknown future or feel defeated by the pressures of today. But You have given me a spirit of power and love. You have given me a sound mind. I find my confidence in You, God. Amen.

Your heavenly Father has put His Holy Spirit in you to comfort you and guide you. Ask Him to do just that today. He will come through. . .every time!

_____

_____

_____

_____

_____

_____

_____

_____

For God hath not given us the spirit of fear;
but of power, and of love, and of a sound mind.

2 TIMOTHY 1:7

Teach Me Thy Paths

Father, I've been guilty of making my own way sometimes without asking You which way to go. I ended up in trouble. Forgive me. Show me the direction to take, and teach me Your ways so I won't get off on the wrong track. I need direction from You. Amen.

God wants to direct our paths if we will only ask Him, receive His instruction, and then follow it.

_____

_____

_____

_____

_____

_____

_____

_____

_____

_____

Shew me thy ways, O LORD; teach me thy paths. Lead me in thy truth, and teach me: for thou art the God of my salvation; on thee do I wait all the day.

PSALM 25:4–5

God Knows Me

God, the Bible says that You knew me even before I was formed in my mother's womb. I find confidence in this. You have been with me all along this journey! As I face this day, help me to remember that I am never alone. You go before me to prepare the future. You walk with me through the present. And You were there with me since before I was born. Wow! Amen.

When a child rides high upon her father's shoulders, she is the queen of the world! Find confidence in the fact that the God of the universe carries you today!

....

....

....

....

....

....

....

....

For thou hast possessed my reins: thou hast covered me in my mother's womb. I will praise thee; for I am fearfully and wonderfully made: marvellous are thy works; and that my soul knoweth right well.

PSALM 139:13–14

Fret Not

Lord, sometimes I get so frustrated because I see people living sinful lives and yet they seem to be successful. It doesn't really seem fair, especially when Christians work so hard to do the right thing and struggle in their daily lives. Help me not to focus on what others are doing, especially those who are living in sin. Help me to focus on Your promises, what You have done for me, and what You are going to do in the future. Amen.

Keep your mind and eyes focused on God and His goodness in your life. Don't be sidetracked by the success of the world. It's a temporary state.

....

....

....

....

....

....

....

....

Fret not thyself because of evildoers, neither be thou envious against the workers of iniquity. For they shall soon be cut down like the grass, and wither as the green herb. Trust in the LORD, and do good; so shalt thou dwell in the land, and verily thou shalt be fed.

PSALM 37:1–3

Taking a Stand

There is nothing in this world that can separate me from Your love!
Father, what strength I find in this promise! As a Christian, I stand out.
At times, no one agrees with the stand I take or the choices I make.
Sometimes it feels like the whole world is on the other side!
Thank You that You are always with me. I face this day
with confidence because You are on my side. Amen.

We read of great men and women of God in the Bible that took a stand for Christ. Sometimes no one else supported them. But God was with them!

....

....

....

....

....

....

....

....

....

Though an host should encamp against me, my heart shall not fear:
though war should rise against me, in this will I be confident.

PSALM 27:3

He Is My Shepherd

Jesus, thank You for being my Shepherd. Without You I would wander around like a lost sheep. You take such good care of me. I don't have to be in want for anything. You've provided all the necessities of life and many extras along with it. Sometimes You have to prod me back into the right pasture, but it's always for my benefit. Amen.

With Jesus as your Shepherd, you will always have what you need. He will find green pastures and still waters for your benefit.

The LORD is my Shepherd; I shall not want. He maketh me to lie down in green pastures: he leadeth me beside the still waters.

PSALM 23:1–2

DAY 163

Facing the Future

Lord, thank You that I don't have to worry about tomorrow. I can face an uncertain future with a certain God at my side. You are all the confidence I need! You have never left me, and You never will. Tomorrow may bring a scary diagnosis, an unthinkable loss, or a deep disappointment. But You will be there holding my hand. You can take care of me through any storm. I love You, Lord. Amen.

Those who worry about the future miss the joy in today! Let your loving heavenly Father handle what is yet to come. Live, love, and laugh today!

Take therefore no thought for the morrow: for the morrow shall take thought for the things of itself. Sufficient unto the day is the evil thereof.
MATTHEW 6:34

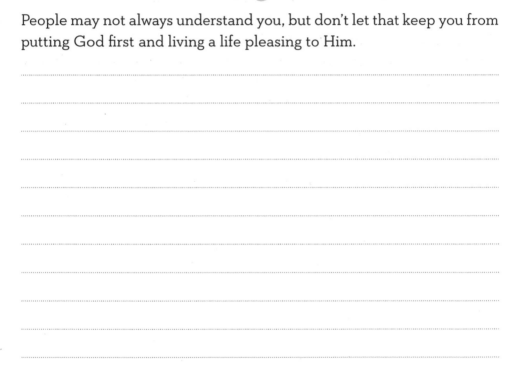

DAY 164

Daughter of God

Father, I'm so thankful that I belong to You. You loved me so much that You gave me the opportunity to become a part of Your family. The world doesn't understand why that is so important to me. They don't know why I've chosen this life instead of worldly pursuits, but I'm glad You know me and I know You. Amen.

People may not always understand you, but don't let that keep you from putting God first and living a life pleasing to Him.

Behold, what manner of love the Father hath bestowed upon us, that we should be called the sons of God: therefore the world knoweth us not, because it knew him not.

1 JOHN 3:1

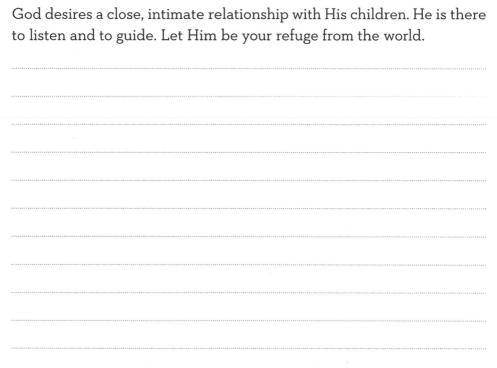

DAY 165
Refuge in Christ

Heavenly Father, there is no place like home. You are my home.
Wherever I go in life and whatever I do, I find my refuge in You.
I come before You now humbly, recognizing that You are the almighty
God of the universe. And yet I can call You Abba Father, my Daddy,
my Protector. Let me face this day with confidence
as a daughter of the King. Amen.

God desires a close, intimate relationship with His children. He is there
to listen and to guide. Let Him be your refuge from the world.

In the fear of the LORD is strong confidence:
and his children shall have a place of refuge.
PROVERBS 14:26

DAY 166

He Lifts Me Up

Lord, when I hear about bad things happening to people, the enemy wants me to become afraid that something might happen to me. I'm so glad that I belong to You. Even though trouble might be on every side, You are my shield. Not only that, but You're the lifter up of my head. You keep me safe, and Your Spirit keeps me from becoming discouraged about trouble. Thank You. Amen.

When it feels as though there is trouble on every hand, the Lord will be a shield unto you and lift up your head when you're down.

....

....

....

....

....

....

....

....

Lord, how are they increased that trouble me! Many are they that rise up against me. Many there be which say of my soul, There is no help for him in God. Selah. But thou, O LORD, art a shield for me; my glory, and the lifter up of mine head.

PSALM 3:1–3

My Help Is in the Lord

Lord, I thank You for all of the leaders and authorities in my life. I thank You for the leaders of my country, state, and city. I pray for those in powerful positions this morning. I pray that they might turn to You and be led by You as they lead others. My ultimate trust is not in anyone but You, Sovereign God. You are my hope. In Jesus' name, amen.

Be confident that regardless of the decisions of earthly leaders, as God's child, you will be protected by His hand.

Put not your trust in princes, nor in the son of man, in whom there is no help.

PSALM 146:3

Envy Not

Lord, touch me by Your Spirit this morning that I will not envy those around me. Your blessing on my life far outweighs whatever the world can give me. Help me to focus on eternal priorities and not on temporal desires that cause me to envy what others have. Help me to walk in Your ways today. Amen.

It's easy to look around and be a little envious of what others are doing or obtaining, but remember that all of those things are only temporary pleasures. Much better things await those who know Christ.

Let not thine heart envy sinners: but be thou in the fear of the LORD all the day long.

PROVERBS 23:17

God Hears My Prayers

Lord, the gods of other religions are not approachable. Their subjects bow before them in anguish, hoping to find favor in their sight. These gods are not real. You are the one true and living God, a loving heavenly Father. I love that Your Word says I can come before You with confidence. You hear my prayers. You know my heart. Thank You, Father. Speak to my heart as I meditate upon Your Word now. Amen.

God loves you so much that He has adopted you into His family through Jesus. Go before Him with the confidence of a beloved daughter.

And this is the confidence that we have in him, that, if we ask any thing according to his will, he heareth us.

1 JOHN 5:14

Ordered by the Lord

Father, order my steps today. I know from experience that when I order my own steps, I end up stumbling around. Wherever my duties take me, help me to walk where You direct me. Don't let me get so busy that I get off the path You've laid out for me. Help me to stay attentive to Your voice and be guided by Your Spirit. Amen.

Allowing God to order our steps puts us on the right path to follow.

The steps of a good man are ordered by the LORD: and he delighteth in his way. Though he fall, he shall not be utterly cast down: for the LORD upholdeth him with his hand.

PSALM 37:23–24

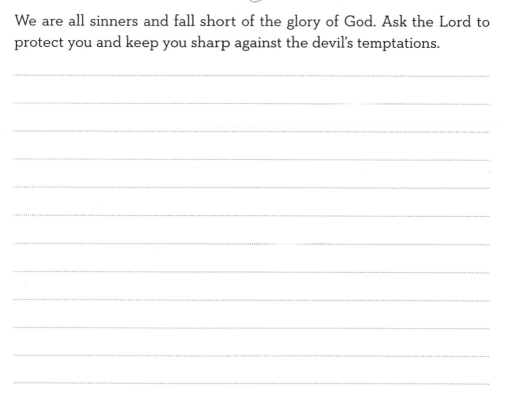

DAY 171

Avoiding Overconfidence

God, it's easy to judge others. It's harder to take a good look at my own life. I find myself thinking, I would never. . . *or* How could she? *What dangerous thoughts! Where I am most confident that I would never fail You, I just might. Your disciple Peter was so sure he would not betray You and yet. . .look what happened. "But for the grace of God go I" should instead be my motto. Amen.*

We are all sinners and fall short of the glory of God. Ask the Lord to protect you and keep you sharp against the devil's temptations.

Wherefore let him that thinketh he standeth take heed lest he fall.
1 CORINTHIANS 10:12

Light for Darkness

God, the world around us is out of control. Your people no longer see things as black and white or right and wrong. Those things we used to call sin are no longer wrong. We think it's okay to do whatever we like because it's our life. Lord, don't let me get caught up in that deception. Help me to discern good from evil and light from darkness. Amen.

If you know something is wrong, stand by your convictions. Don't allow the world around you to influence your knowledge of right and wrong.

*Woe unto them that call evil good, and good evil;
that put darkness for light, and light for darkness;
that put bitter for sweet, and sweet for bitter!*

ISAIAH 5:20

DAY 173
More like Jesus

Lord, sometimes I feel so inadequate. I fail at the very things I strive to do well in my life. I feel like the apostle Paul who said that he did the very things he tried not to do. Thank You for the promise that You aren't through with me yet! I am confident that You will continue to teach and grow me. Make me more like Jesus each passing day, I pray. Amen.

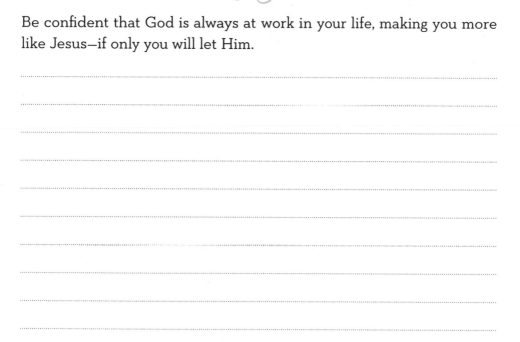

Be confident that God is always at work in your life, making you more like Jesus—if only you will let Him.

Being confident of this very thing, that he which hath begun a good work in you will perform it until the day of Jesus Christ.
PHILIPPIANS 1:6

According to His Will

Father, a lot of my prayers are requests that You do something for me or my family and friends. I don't always get the answer I prayed for, but I know that You hear me. Maybe one of the reasons I don't get an answer is I didn't pray according to Your will. Thank You for hearing me when I pray, and help me to pray according to Your will and not mine. Amen.

What do your prayers sound like? Are they all requests for your own desires, or do you pray for God's will?

_____

_____

_____

_____

_____

_____

_____

_____

And this is the confidence that we have in him, that, if we ask any thing according to his will, he heareth us: and if we know that he hear us, whatsoever we ask, we know that we have the petitions that we desired of him.

1 JOHN 5:14–15

Always with Me

God, You have put some great people in my life. Sometimes I feel afraid that something will happen to one of them or that I will be left alone. Remind me, Lord, that You are always with me. You will be with me even if I face a great loss. You will not leave me. Help me to enjoy each day with my loved ones and not to fear the future. Amen.

Even if you lose the dearest loves of your life, God will be there with you. You are never alone.

_____

_____

_____

_____

_____

_____

_____

_____

_____

_____

Be strong and of a good courage, fear not, nor be afraid of them: for the LORD thy God, he it is that doth go with thee; he will not fail thee, nor forsake thee.

DEUTERONOMY 31:6

A Faithful Daughter-in-Law

Father, when Ruth followed Naomi back to her homeland, it was all a part of Your plan. Ruth met Boaz; they married and had a son, Obed, who was grandfather to David. From the line of David came Jesus, who brought salvation to us. What a wonderful plan. Lord, keep me open to Your plans for my life. You know what's best for me if I follow Your leading. Amen.

You may not understand the way God is working in your life, but He has a plan for you. Trust Him to do the best for you.

_____

_____

_____

_____

_____

_____

_____

_____

_____

_____

And Ruth said, Intreat me not to leave thee, or to return from following after thee: for whither thou goest, I will go; and where thou lodgest, I will lodge: thy people shall be my people, and thy God my God.

RUTH 1:16

More Than a Conqueror

Father, You tell me in Your Word that I am more than a conqueror.
I ponder these words. What do they mean? I am more than a
conqueror. I am a winner. I am a chosen child of the almighty God.
I am a victor. I shall see You one day. I have an abundant life
and an eternal one. I am more than a conqueror.
I shall walk in Your strength, Father. Amen.

God doesn't just want His people to survive. He wants us to lead abundant, joy-filled lives. He calls us more than conquerors!

Nay, in all these things we are more than
conquerors through him that loved us.
ROMANS 8:37

Rock of Salvation

God, how wonderful to know that You are my rock of salvation. A rock is solid and strong. I can count on You when storms rock my world. I know You'll be there. That is so comforting when winds of trouble are blowing and all around me foundations are crumbling. Thank You for being my rock. Amen.

When God is the rock of your salvation, you can rest assured your foundation is strong.

_____

_____

_____

_____

_____

_____

_____

_____

_____

_____

_____

The LORD liveth; and blessed be my rock;
and exalted be the God of the rock of my salvation.

2 SAMUEL 22:47

Wisdom from God

Father, the world does not have wisdom to offer me. True wisdom comes only from You. Help me today to walk as a wise daughter of the sovereign King of kings. Keep me from the temptation to listen to what the world calls wisdom. Even in times such as these, there is a remnant of Your people. We will be known by our love and by the wisdom we possess. Amen.

The ways of the world are not the ways of the Father. Seek God. Find true wisdom.

See then that ye walk circumspectly, not as fools, but as wise, redeeming the time, because the days are evil.

EPHESIANS 5:15–16

Cease from Anger

Father, forgive me for the words I spoke in anger. Looking back on what I said makes me ashamed. Anger makes us do and say things we shouldn't. Sometimes we're angry because we're hurt, but sometimes it's because we want to hurt someone else, and that's wrong. Direct my thoughts so I will think before I speak and not have any desire to say or do something evil. Amen.

Don't allow anger to dictate what you say and how you act. The consequences are painful.

Cease from anger, and forsake wrath: fret not thyself in any wise to do evil. For evildoers shall be cut off: but those that wait upon the LORD, they shall inherit the earth.

PSALM 37:8–9

Wise Counsel

Help me, Lord, to know when I need to seek counsel from others. I don't want to step out, as I sometimes have in the past, on my own. I want to walk in Your ways and in Your will. Sometimes we all need help. Guide me to someone who is grounded in Your Word so that any counsel I receive will be truth. Give me wisdom, I pray. Amen.

Younger believers should seek counsel from those who have been following Jesus longer. God has put such people in your life for a reason.

The way of a fool is right in his own eyes: but he that hearkeneth unto counsel is wise.

PROVERBS 12:15

God Passes the Test

God, when Elijah offered a sacrifice to You in the presence of 450 prophets of Baal, he trusted You to come through victorious. Let me have that same faith. Help me not to be afraid to trust You. You will always pass the test. Whatever I face today, help me to offer it to You and trust that You will give me victory. Amen.

Trust God with your biggest problems. He will always pass the test.

Then the fire of the LORD fell, and consumed the burnt sacrifice, and the wood, and the stones, and the dust, and licked up the water that was in the trench. And when all the people saw it, they fell on their faces: and they said, The LORD, he is the God; the LORD, he is the God.

1 KINGS 18:38–39

Applying Instruction

God, give me ears to hear. Sharpen my senses and make me wise. I am often proud. I think I know it all. But I don't. I need instruction from You. I know this comes in many forms. . .through reading and meditating on Your Word, through Your people, and through circumstances. Help me to be a good listener and to apply the instruction You send my way. I want to be wise, Father. Amen.

Hearing and listening are two very different things. The truly wise believer will apply the instruction he or she is given. Listening well will serve you well.

Hear counsel, and receive instruction,
that thou mayest be wise in thy latter end.
PROVERBS 19:20

He Will Sustain You

Lord, when I've gone just about as far as I can go, help me to carry on.
When my burden gets to be more than I can carry, give me strength.
You know my limits. When I need to lean on You for support,
I'm so thankful I can give my burden to You
and You will see me through. Amen.

You don't have to carry that load all by yourself. Give it to Jesus, and He will carry it for you.

Cast thy burden upon the Lord, and he shall sustain thee:
he shall never suffer the righteous to be moved.

PSALM 55:22

When to Remain Silent

*Heavenly Father, Your Word says that the tongue has great power.
My words can help or harm. There are times when silence is best.
Help me to know the difference between times I should speak and
times I should keep still. I pray for wisdom as I go through this day. I
want my speech to honor You. Put a guard over my lips, I pray. Amen.*

Words can encourage or discourage. They can build trust or they can build
divisive walls. Choose your words wisely. Ask God to guide you in this.

*In the multitude of words there wanteth not sin:
but he that refraineth his lips is wise.*

PROVERBS 10:19

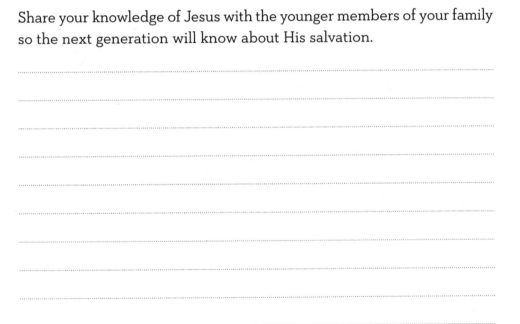

Make Known His Faithfulness

God, Your mercies are so great toward Your people. I've experienced Your mercy in my own life. Help me to share what You've done for me with those around me, especially those in my family. Let me speak of Your faithfulness without reservation. If I don't spread the word to the younger ones in my family, who will? Help me to do my part to make You known to them. Amen.

Share your knowledge of Jesus with the younger members of your family so the next generation will know about His salvation.

_____

_____

_____

_____

_____

_____

_____

_____

_____

I will sing of the mercies of the LORD for ever: with my mouth will I make known thy faithfulness to all generations.

PSALM 89:1

A Wise Woman

God, others look to me as an example. I am a leader whether I want to be or not. I set the tone in my home. Give me grace and patience. Teach me how to build a home with a strong foundation rather than one that collapses when the storms come. Make my resistance strong against Satan, who tempts me to argue and isolate. Instead, find me to be a peacemaker in my home. Amen.

God loves you. He wants your home to be a great success! Rely on Him daily to lead you as you seek to build your home on a wise foundation.

Every wise woman buildeth her house:
but the foolish plucketh it down with her hands.

PROVERBS 14:1

Don't Waste Time

Lord, we don't know when our days are over. We could be young or old when we meet You. But whatever time I have, help me not to waste it. Show me what I need to do to redeem the time for You. Help me to live my life in a way that pleases You. Give me wisdom to make the most of my time. Amen.

Life is a precious gift. Use it to glorify God.

*So teach us to number our days,
that we may apply our hearts unto wisdom.*

PSALM 90:12

A Calm Spirit

Lord Jesus, I read in the Bible of the times that You expressed anger. They were few and far between. It was a righteous anger, a godly anger over great offenses to Your Father. I, on the other hand, sometimes have a short fuse. I want to be wise. Fool is a strong word. Your Word says that to have a hot temper is foolish. Replace my anger with even-tempered responses, I pray. Amen.

In your own strength, you will not be able to maintain a calm spirit. With God's help, it is possible. Lean on His strength. He wants to help you.

A fool uttereth all his mind:
but a wise man keepeth it in till afterwards.
PROVERBS 29:11

A Present Help

Lord, the nightly news is filled with tragedy and evil acts. Man is set on committing evil. Even the environment is chaotic with horrific storms—tornados, hurricanes, fires. If I allow myself to dwell on these things, I can become fearful. I'm glad I know that You are my refuge, a very present help. Thank You for being my protection in the time of trouble. Amen.

When trouble is all around you, focus on God. He is your refuge and strength.

God is our refuge and strength, a very present help in trouble. Therefore will not we fear, though the earth be removed, and though the mountains be carried into the midst of the sea; though the waters thereof roar and be troubled, though the mountains shake with the swelling thereof. Selah.

PSALM 46:1–3

Godly Wisdom

Lord, there are so many self-help books out there now. There are even therapists on TV who claim to have all the answers for our problems. Not to mention the opinions of my friends and family members! I read in Your Word that You were the One who put the wisdom in Solomon's heart. Open my eyes that I may see. I want the wisdom of God Almighty. Grant me wisdom, I pray. Amen.

When you exhibit the wisdom of God, others will come to you for counsel. Be ready to give an answer. Be ready to share godly wisdom.

And all the kings of the earth sought the presence of Solomon, to hear his wisdom, that God had put in his heart.

2 CHRONICLES 9:23

DAY 192

He Holds My Hand

Father, it's nice to have someone hold my hand. It makes me feel secure. It's so comforting to know that You care about me, and when I'm down or feeling defeated, You reach out and take my hand and walk with me through whatever valley I'm facing. I don't have to be afraid as long as we're walking together. Amen.

You don't have to walk alone. God will hold your hand and walk beside you.

For I the LORD thy God will hold thy right hand, saying unto thee, Fear not; I will help thee.

ISAIAH 41:13

Fear of the Lord

Lord, there is no greater One than You. I come before You this morning as Your daughter, and yet I must not let the fact that You are my Abba Father (Daddy) negate Your holiness. You are set apart. You are good. You are all that I am not in my humanity. I am humbled, and I revere You. May my fear of the Lord be the beginning of wisdom in my spirit. Amen.

Simply by fearing the Lord, honoring Him, declaring Him holy, you have begun on your journey toward great wisdom. Honor Him in all that you do and say today.

And unto man he said, Behold, the fear of the LORD, that is wisdom; and to depart from evil is understanding.

JOB 28:28

He Knows My Name

Lord, I meet people on the street who are complete strangers. I don't know their names. We might share a greeting or a smile, but I don't really know them. I'm so glad You know my name. You know me like no one else does. I'm not just a stranger on the street or a population statistic to You. I belong to You. Thank You for that privilege. Amen.

You're no stranger to God. He knows your name and where you live. You belong to Him and He cares about you.

But now thus saith the LORD that created thee, O Jacob, and he that formed thee, O Israel, Fear not: for I have redeemed thee, I have called thee by thy name; thou art mine.

ISAIAH 43:1

Right Paths

The right path is often the one less traveled. I am learning this, Father, oh so slowly. You will always lead me in the right path. You will never lead me astray. I have been at the crossroads many times, and I will face such choices again and again. Keep my heart focused on You that I might be led down pleasant paths, paths that will glorify my King. Amen.

When you reach a fork in the road and you are not sure which path to take, stop. There is always time to pray. God will direct your heart.

I have taught thee in the way of wisdom;
I have led thee in right paths.

PROVERBS 4:11

Sin Separates

God, I don't want anything to come between You and me.
Sometimes I go off on my own agenda and forget temporarily
what I'm supposed to be doing. That's when I get in trouble.
I'm tempted at times to let my flesh take over because it looks
good. That's always a mistake. I'm sorry for any sin that might
be in my life. I don't want anything to separate You and me. Amen.

Sin separates you from God. It may feel good or look good for a while, but it will keep you from having a relationship with Him.

....

....

....

....

....

....

....

....

But your iniquities have separated between you and your God,
and your sins have hid his face from you, that he will not hear.
ISAIAH 59:2

God's Counsel Is Eternal

Lord, I wish my heart was always in tune with Yours. I wish that I did not experience temptations to stray from Your perfect plan. But in truth, I struggle. There is a force within me that is fleshly and human. I feel pulled in the wrong direction at times. I know that Your counsel is eternal. It is a strong foundation on which I want to build my life. Strengthen me, I pray. Amen.

God understands that you are human. Ever since the fall in the garden, sin has been part of the equation. Ask Him for strength. He will provide it.

There are many devices in a man's heart; nevertheless the counsel of the LORD, that shall stand.

PROVERBS 19:21

Be Not Afraid

God, I'm not a fan of speaking to crowds. I'm a nervous wreck waiting for the time to arrive, and then when it does, my voice quivers and I shake. I always wonder what they think of me. But according to Your Word, I don't have to feel that way. I don't have to be afraid. You will give me courage. I claim that victory today. Amen.

You don't have to be afraid to stand before people. God has promised to help you.

....

....

....

....

....

....

....

....

....

....

*Be not afraid of their faces: for I am
with thee to deliver thee, saith the LORD.*
JEREMIAH 1:8

Grant Me Wisdom

Lord, give me wisdom. I ask for wisdom from the one true God,
the wise One, the all-knowing, omnipotent One. You are the Giver of
all knowledge. You are the Way, the Truth, and the Life. In You, I find
the answers to life's puzzling questions. I seek You, and I find You.
As I meditate upon Your Word, instruct me, I pray.
I ask these things in Jesus' name, amen.

God wants to give you wisdom. He blessed Solomon with great wisdom.
He will instruct you if you will seek Him. Be still before Him. . .and listen.

And God gave Solomon wisdom and understanding exceeding much,
and largeness of heart, even as the sand that is on the sea shore.
And Solomon's wisdom excelled the wisdom of all the children
of the east country, and all the wisdom of Egypt.

1 KINGS 4:29–30

Create, Renew, Restore

Lord, the psalmist asks for a clean heart and a right spirit. He wanted to live in Your presence and experience the joy of salvation. I want those same things for myself. Clean up my heart, and renew Your Spirit within me. Help me to walk in Your presence every day. Restore unto me the joy I felt when I first met You. Amen.

Let God do a work of renewal and restoration in you today. Experience the joy of salvation.

Create in me a clean heart, O God; and renew a right spirit within me. Cast me not away from thy presence; and take not thy holy spirit from me. Restore unto me the joy of thy salvation; and uphold me with thy free spirit.

PSALM 51:10–12

Amazing Grace

Lord, I get so caught up in trying to do good works sometimes. I need to remember that I am saved by grace. You are pleased with me simply because I believe in Your Son, Jesus, and I have accepted Him as my Savior. You do not bless me or withhold good gifts based on my performance. Remind me of Your amazing grace, and make me gracious with others. In Jesus' name, I pray, amen.

"Grace, grace. . . God's grace. . . Grace that is greater than all our sin. . ." Rest in the calm assurance that you are saved by grace through faith in Christ Jesus.

For by grace are ye saved through faith; and that not of yourselves: it is the gift of God: not of works, lest any man should boast.
EPHESIANS 2:8–9

Remember the Lord

Father, when You spoke to Jonah about going to Nineveh, he ran the other way. I confess that I've been guilty of that a time or two. It's not because I don't want to be obedient; it's because I'm afraid and feel unqualified. Whatever the reason, when Jonah ran, he got into serious trouble. Give me the courage I need to run toward You and what You require of me. Amen.

If God requires you to do a job, do not be afraid. He qualifies those He calls. Remember He loves you and will be with you each step of the way.

....

....

....

....

....

....

....

When my soul fainted within me I remembered the LORD: and my prayer came in unto thee, into thine holy temple. . . . But I will sacrifice unto thee with the voice of thanksgiving; I will pay that that I have vowed. Salvation is of the LORD.

JONAH 2:7, 9

Grace with Others

Jesus, You came to earth to live among us. You were fully God and yet fully man. You were, as the book of John says, "full of grace and truth." May I follow Your example. May I be found full of grace and truth. Give me a gracious, forgiving spirit. Grant me the discernment to see Your truth, Your light even amid the darkness of the world. Thank You, Lord. Amen.

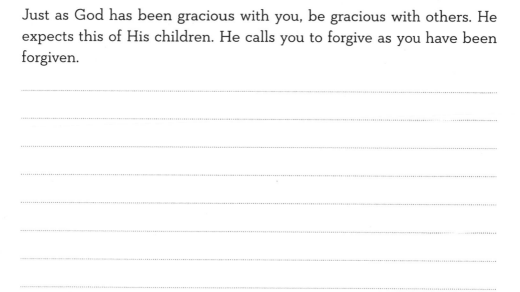

Just as God has been gracious with you, be gracious with others. He expects this of His children. He calls you to forgive as you have been forgiven.

And the Word was made flesh, and dwelt among us, (and we beheld his glory, the glory as of the only begotten of the Father,) full of grace and truth.

JOHN 1:14

Give God Your Heart

Father, I give You my heart this morning. I'm already Your child, but I want You to have access to all of me. If there are hidden motives, thoughts, or issues, please forgive me. Help me to turn my eyes upon You and observe Your ways that I may live a life pleasing to You. I desire a closer walk with You. Amen.

Giving God your heart is much more than just repeating words. It means opening yourself up to His examination and allowing Him to change you completely.

My son, give me thine heart, and let thine eyes observe my ways.

PROVERBS 23:26

A Messenger of Grace

Lord, make me a messenger of grace and peace. When I enter a room and when I leave it, may grace and peace be the mark that I was there. Season my conversations with these positive elements. Remove all malice and gossip from my thoughts and speech. Help me to be more like Jesus. I want to be a peacemaker. I want to be known as gracious. Amen.

The apostle Paul often began and ended his letters by offering a blessing of grace and peace. Do you bless others' lives with grace and peace?

Grace be to you and peace from God our Father, and from the Lord Jesus Christ.

2 CORINTHIANS 1:2

The Whole Matter

God, my whole duty is to fear You and keep Your commandments. I try my best to do this, but if there is some area in which I fail to please You, please show me. It's easy for us to see where someone else falls short, but not so with ourselves. We can't see our own shortcomings, so please show me where I need to improve. Amen.

It's easy to see someone else's faults, but we're blind to our own. Ask God to show you if there's an area where you need to improve.

....

....

....

....

....

....

....

....

....

....

Let us hear the conclusion of the whole matter: Fear God, and keep his commandments: for this is the whole duty of man.

ECCLESIASTES 12:13

Steward of Grace

Thank You for the gifts You have given me, Lord. I look around at the other believers in my life. We are all gifted in different ways. Help me to be a good steward of the gifts You have entrusted me with in this life. Instead of looking out for myself, give me opportunities to use my abilities to minister to others. I understand that it is in doing so that I honor You. Amen.

The world would be boring if everyone looked alike. And what if we all had the same gifts and abilities? Instead, we work together as one body with many parts.

As every man hath received the gift, even so minister the same one to another, as good stewards of the manifold grace of God.

1 PETER 4:10

He Goes Before Us

Lord, I need Your direction today. I don't know what lies ahead of me, but You do. There may be twists and turns in my path to distract me or cause me pain, but with Your direction, I can avoid these obstacles. Go before me and make the crooked places straight that I will not be diverted from the path You have chosen for me. Amen.

Start your day by asking God for direction. He knows what lies ahead of you.

_____

_____

_____

_____

_____

_____

_____

_____

_____

_____

_____

I will go before thee, and make the crooked places straight: I will break in pieces the gates of brass, and cut in sunder the bars of iron.

ISAIAH 45:2

Unmerited Favor

Jesus, the word grace sounds so sweet. But when I see You on that cross, bleeding, aching, dying an excruciating death, it takes on a new depth, a new meaning. You tasted death for me. You took my place. That is the grace of God. That is unmerited favor. That is unexplainable, unfathomable, and yet. . .true. Oh Jesus, thank You for Your grace. Thank You for dying for me. I will live for You. Amen.

Gaze at Jesus as He hangs upon the cross. That is the picture of grace. That is the epitome of mercy and love exemplified in your Savior.

But we see Jesus, who was made a little lower than the angels for the suffering of death, crowned with glory and honour; that he by the grace of God should taste death for every man.

HEBREWS 2:9

Great Faith

Jesus, when the centurion asked You to heal his servant who was sick, You were ready to go to his house and heal the servant. But the centurion felt unworthy to have You in his house. He said, "Just speak the word and it will be done." You called it great faith. Jesus, I want that kind of faith. Faith that knows all You have to do is speak it and it happens. Increase my faith, Lord. Amen.

Stretch your faith to believe that Jesus can do the impossible in your life.

The centurion answered and said, Lord, I am not worthy that thou shouldest come under my roof: but speak the word only, and my servant shall be healed. . . . When Jesus heard it, he marvelled, and said to them that followed, Verily I say unto you, I have not found so great faith, no, not in Israel.

MATTHEW 8:8, 10

Under Grace

I am different because of grace, Father. Your free gift of salvation changes things. It sets me free. It gives me life and light and glorious joy that cannot be stolen from me. I do not have to bow to sin. It will not rule in my life. I live under the grace of Your Son, Jesus Christ. I choose to live for You and through You all of my days. Amen.

The law was not abolished by grace, but grace made a way for us. Grace is a bridge. Step onto it. Trust it. Find your way to the Father through grace.

For sin shall not have dominion over you:
for ye are not under the law, but under grace.

ROMANS 6:14

We Are the Clay

Lord, on those days when everything seems to go wrong and I feel totally useless, cause me to remember that we all are the work of Thy hand. You created us in Your image. We don't have to feel useless. You created us for a purpose. I'm just a piece of clay who needs to be molded by You into a useful vessel. Amen.

Allow God to mold you into the image of Him.

_____

_____

_____

_____

_____

_____

_____

_____

_____

_____

But now, O LORD, thou art our father; we are the clay, and thou our potter; and we all are the work of thy hand.
ISAIAH 64:8

The Cross Covers Sin

God, I recognize daily that this is a fallen world. With one bite of fruit in the garden called Eden, we fell from grace. Sin entered the world. We were separated from our Creator. I turn from that garden scene to another scene called Calvary. What a contrast. What a gift. Grace with skin on. Grace that wore a crown of thorns and bled and died for mankind. Thank You, Jesus, for Your grace. Amen.

The sin of one brought death to all mankind. The death of Another offers life. The cross of Christ covers that bite of forbidden fruit. . .and it covers your sin. Receive the blessing.

For if by one man's offence death reigned by one; much more they which receive abundance of grace and of the gift of righteousness shall reign in life by one, Jesus Christ.
ROMANS 5:17

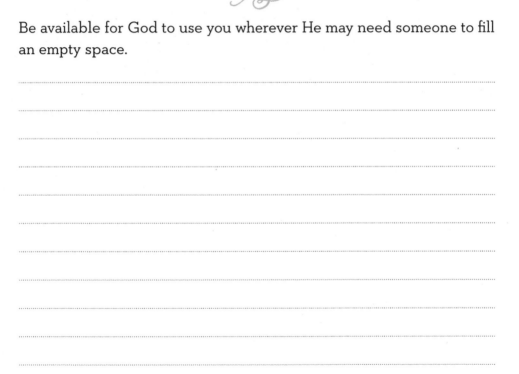

Stand in the Gap

*God, I'm just one person with limited abilities, but I know all things
are possible with You. Through You I can be the person who stands
in the gap for others and their needs. I can make up the hedge
where there is a hole that needs to be filled. Guide me into
the places where You want me to make up the gap. Amen.*

Be available for God to use you wherever He may need someone to fill
an empty space.

_____

_____

_____

_____

_____

_____

_____

_____

_____

*And I sought for a man among them, that should make up the
hedge, and stand in the gap before me for the land,
that I should not destroy it: but I found none.*

 EZEKIEL 22:30

Not by Works

I cannot earn salvation, can I, Father? This life is packed with working and earning. Hard work often equals success or reward. But with You, there is unmerited favor. There is the gift of salvation offered to me as just that, a gift. For what kind of God would You be if You offered a gift and asked for payment in return? I am saved by the great fullness of grace and grace alone. Amen.

If you stacked up all your good works, wouldn't you also have a sin stack to present to God? Not even one sin can come before Him. It is by grace you are saved and not by works.

And if by grace, then is it no more of works: otherwise grace is no more grace. But if it be of works, then it is no more grace: otherwise work is no more work.

ROMANS 11:6

A New Spirit

*Lord, give me a new spirit. The one I have now is self-centered,
thinking only of myself and what I desire. Give me a spirit of peace,
love, and grace that others can be touched by You working through me.
Put within me a spirit that comes from You, not one of my own making,
which is often grumpy, moody, and disagreeable. Amen.*

Take some time to think about your spirit. What is it like? Would it be
the kind of spirit that God would place within you?

_____

_____

_____

_____

_____

_____

_____

_____

*A new heart also will I give you, and a new spirit will I put within you:
and I will take away the stony heart out of your flesh, and I will give
you an heart of flesh. And I will put my spirit within you, and cause you
to walk in my statutes, and ye shall keep my judgments, and do them.*

EZEKIEL 36:26–27

Extravagant Grace

Father, You poured out Your grace. The gift of Your Son was an extravagant gift. It was of deep and painful cost to You, and yet You gave it with reckless abandon. You didn't think twice. Often I am stingy with grace. I sprinkle it. I offer it in drips or tiny tastes. I want to be generous with grace. I want it to overflow from my life. Change my heart, I pray. Amen.

When a believer truly begins to grasp the grace of God, he or she will offer grace more freely to others. It is a natural outgrowth of salvation.

*And the grace of our Lord was exceeding abundant
with faith and love which is in Christ Jesus.*
1 TIMOTHY 1:14

Wait on God

Father, sometimes I'm impatient. Maybe it's the flesh acting up or maybe it's because we live in an instant-gratification world where everything happens at the push of a button or the touch of a finger on a screen. Whatever the cause, I need to wait on You instead of trying to do things on my own. Help me to wait on You continually. Amen.

We think we know best, but we are mistaken. Waiting on God is always to our benefit. He sees the big picture. We see only the present.

Therefore turn thou to thy God: keep mercy and judgment and wait on thy God continually.

HOSEA 12:6

An Heir to the King

Heavenly Father, thank You for adopting me as an heir to the King of kings! You provided a way for me to come before You, Holy God. Christ carried my sin as His burden. It was nailed to the cross and has been forgiven forever, once and for all. Thank You for the abundant life that is mine because I am Yours. I praise You for viewing me through a lens called grace. Amen.

When God looks at you, He sees you through a "Jesus lens." He sees you as righteous and pure because His Son resides in your heart.

That being justified by his grace, we should be made heirs according to the hope of eternal life.

TITUS 3:7

Follow Him

Jesus, You called fishermen and a tax collector, men looked down on by society, to follow You, and they didn't hesitate. I've been guilty of wondering about people You have called to work for You. It's really none of my business. You can use anyone and qualify them to do the job You have for them. You've done it for me. Thank You for the privilege of following You. Help me not to hesitate when I hear Your voice. Amen.

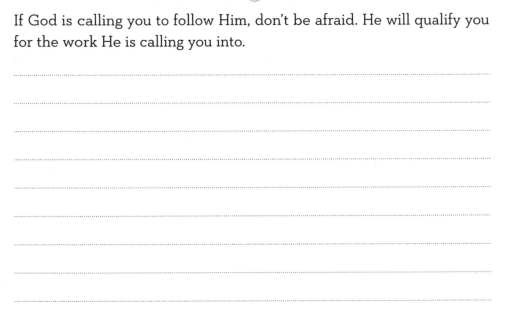

If God is calling you to follow Him, don't be afraid. He will qualify you for the work He is calling you into.

And as Jesus passed forth from thence, he saw a man, named Matthew, sitting at the receipt of custom: and he saith unto him, Follow me. And he arose, and followed him.

MATTHEW 9:9

Loving My Enemies

*Lord, some of Your commands are easy to understand, such as taking
care of widows and orphans. But some of them go against human
nature. It's easier to show mercy to those we love, but You tell us to love
our enemies. You command us to love those who are hard to love.
Give me a love for the unlovable, Father. I want to
have a heart that pleases You. Amen.*

God loves you on your worst day just as much as He loves you when you
are at your best. Extend grace to others. Practice unconditional mercy.

*For if ye love them which love you, what reward have ye? do not
even the publicans the same? And if ye salute your brethren only,
what do ye more than others? do not even the publicans so?*

MATTHEW 5:46–47

God Is Able to Deliver

Father, give me the determination of Shadrach, Meshach, and Abednego. These three men stood firm for You in the face of danger. Their lives were threatened, yet they didn't budge. When they were thrown in the fiery furnace, You were there with them, just as You will be with me when I am faced with danger or threats. Thank You for this amazing example of Your faithfulness. Amen.

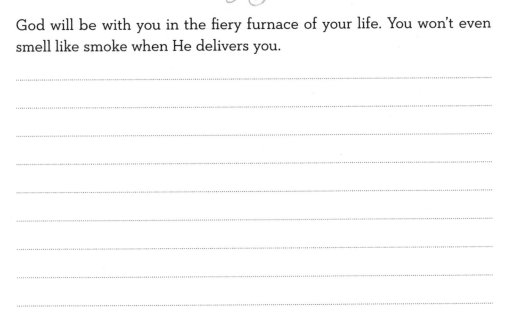

God will be with you in the fiery furnace of your life. You won't even smell like smoke when He delivers you.

And the princes, governors, and captains, and the king's counsellors, being gathered together, saw these men, upon whose bodies the fire had no power, nor was an hair of their head singed, neither were their coats changed, nor the smell of fire had passed on them.

DANIEL 3:27

God Will Be with You

Father, thank You for the promise of Your care and protection. It's so good to know that when we face heartache and trouble, You will be with us. No matter what that situation may be, there is nothing that You can't see us through. You didn't promise to take us out of the problem, but You will be with us through it all. Thank You. Amen.

We may face heartache and trouble, but God will walk through the fire with us, and we can come through with no smell of smoke.

_____
_____
_____
_____
_____
_____
_____
_____
_____

When thou passest through the waters, I will be with thee; and through the rivers, they shall not overflow thee: when thou walkest through the fire, thou shalt not be burned; neither shall the flame kindle upon thee.

ISAIAH 43:2

No Eye Has Seen

Father, my heart rejoices when I think of how much You love me and what You are preparing for Your children. You've blessed us with so many good things here on earth, but I know they can't compare to what You have made ready for us in eternity. Thank You for loving me so much that You sent Your Son to die for me, and now You're preparing a place for us. Amen.

We have been blessed with so many wonderful things here on earth, but they can't compare to what God has prepared for us in the future.

For since the beginning of the world men have not heard, nor perceived by the ear, neither hath the eye seen, O God, beside thee, what he hath prepared for him that waiteth for him.

ISAIAH 64:4

Finding Hope in Scripture

Thank You, heavenly Father, for Your holy Word. The scriptures, which were inspired by You and written long ago, remain today. As I read and meditate upon scripture today, I ask that You fill me with hope. Comfort me through Your Word. Encourage my spirit. Strengthen me for the tasks that lie ahead today. And instruct me in the ways You would have me go. Amen.

The Bible is not just an old book. It is filled with God-breathed, holy words of instruction and comfort. Find hope in God's Word today.

For whatsoever things were written aforetime were written for our learning, that we through patience and comfort of the scriptures might have hope.

ROMANS 15:4

By His Spirit

Father, do a new work in my life by Your Spirit. I need a supernatural experience in my being, an experience that only You can do. Man can't help me in this situation. It's not done by might or strength, power or human invention; it's accomplished by Your Spirit. You have promised this in Your Word and I claim it as one of Your children. Amen.

Some things can only be accomplished in our lives by God's Spirit. Ask Him to do those things for you by His Spirit.

....

....

....

....

....

....

....

....

....

Then he answered and spake unto me, saying, This is the word of the LORD unto Zerubbabel, saying, Not by might, nor by power, but by my spirit, saith the LORD of hosts.

ZECHARIAH 4:6

Reason to Hope

God, this world seems hopeless. People let me down. They are only human. I let them down as well. Life brings disappointments and rejections. I am thankful that You are faithful and true. You are not like men and women. What You say You will do, You always do. You are true to Your Word. You have said that I am Your child and that You will never leave me. You are my hope! Amen.

God does not lie. It is not in His character to do so. Therefore, you can bank on every promise in the Bible. Claim some of them today!

God is not a man, that he should lie; neither the son of man, that he should repent: hath he said, and shall he not do it? or hath he spoken, and shall he not make it good?

Numbers 23:19

Speak Truth

Lord, let me speak Your truth when I open my mouth. Sometimes I say things that do not bring You glory. You have given us specific instructions about the things You want us to do, such as speaking truth to our neighbors, not imagining evil against our neighbor, and executing truth and peace in our homes. Give me the desire to pursue these things that You require of me. Amen.

God is concerned with how we treat our neighbors and those we come in contact with. He doesn't even want us to think bad toward them.

These are the things that ye shall do; Speak ye every man the truth to his neighbour; execute the judgment of truth and peace in your gates: and let none of you imagine evil in your hearts against his neighbour; and love no false oath: for all these are things that I hate, saith the LORD.

ZECHARIAH 8:16–17

Hope in God

Heavenly Father, when I lose my hope, You restore it. When I am depressed, You bring the smile back to my face. Even when my circumstances are not quite as I would wish, I will "yet praise" You, as did the psalmist. I will choose to hope in Christ Jesus. Quiet my soul, Father. Restore health to my countenance. I will yet praise You. I will find hope in Your promises. Amen.

Jesus understands that life is not easy. He lived here on earth Himself! He is always here, ready to comfort you through His presence and His Word. Find hope in Christ today.

_____

_____

_____

_____

_____

_____

_____

_____

Why art thou cast down, O my soul? and why art thou disquieted within me? hope in God: for I shall yet praise him, who is the health of my countenance, and my God.

PSALM 43:5

Vessel unto Honor

Jesus, You saved me and chose me to be a vessel for You. I'm so honored to work for You, but sometimes I feel so unworthy of the tasks You give me. Who am I to be called a vessel of Christ? Your Word tells me that there are vessels of honor and vessels of dishonor. Lord, my desire is to be a vessel of honor for You. Sanctify me that I might be a vessel for Your use, prepared unto good works. Amen.

Our lifestyles reflect whether we are a vessel of honor or dishonor. What does your lifestyle reflect?

....

....

....

....

....

....

....

....

....

....

If a man therefore purge himself from these, he shall be a vessel unto honour, sanctified, and meet for the master's use, and prepared unto every good work.

2 TIMOTHY 2:21

Rejoice in Hope

Lord, I rejoice in hope. I will be patient in tribulations. I will pray constantly. I will follow this guide from Your Word. I know that this is what You desire for me as Your child. You want me to have an abundant, joyful life in Christ. You want me to trust You as trials come into my life. And You desire an intimate relationship with me that is nurtured through prayer. Amen.

God calls us to rejoice in hope, to be patient in times of trial, and to pray at all times. Release your burdens to Him. He is a big God.

Rejoicing in hope; patient in tribulation; continuing instant in prayer.

ROMANS 12:12

An Heir with Christ

God, thank You so much for the inheritance that You have promised those who are born into Your family by receiving Your Son as their Savior. Without Your promise and Your love for us, we would be in spiritual poverty, without hope of eternal life, which is our promised inheritance. Thank You for adopting me into Your family. Amen.

❧

You are a daughter of the King and a joint heir with Christ of God's promised inheritance.

_____

_____

_____

_____

_____

_____

_____

_____

But when the fulness of the time was come, God sent forth his Son, made of a woman, made under the law, to redeem them that were under the law, that we might receive the adoption of sons. . . . Wherefore thou art no more a servant, but a son; and if a son, then an heir of God through Christ.

GALATIANS 4:4–5, 7

A Testimony of Hope

God, hopeful people stand out in a hopeless world. When others notice my ability to face trials without giving up, may I give a reason for it. That reason is You. Without my faith, I would be lost and without any hope. With it, I am able to maintain an inner joy even in the midst of tough situations. May my life be a testimony to the hope found only in Christ Jesus! Amen.

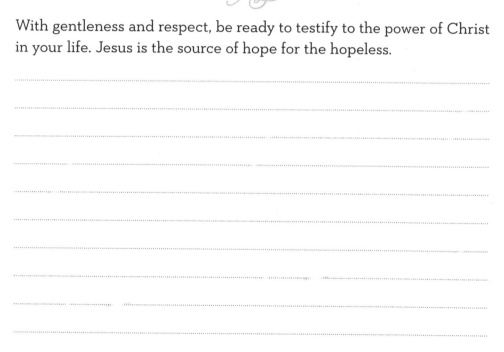

With gentleness and respect, be ready to testify to the power of Christ in your life. Jesus is the source of hope for the hopeless.

But sanctify the Lord God in your hearts: and be ready always to give an answer to every man that asketh you a reason of the hope that is in you with meekness and fear.

1 PETER 3:15

Put on the Armor

Jesus, You've supplied me with what I need to fight the enemy, but it's up to me to put it on every morning. I'm not strong enough by myself to fight against spiritual wickedness. But You've given me armor to protect me against the attack of the enemy. Give me the strength to put it on every morning and then do all I can to stand for You, knowing You are fighting right beside me. Amen.

As a woman, we take care with our hair, makeup, and dress, but as a Christian, we must not consider ourselves complete unless we have on the armor of God.

_____

_____

_____

_____

_____

_____

_____

_____

_____

Wherefore take unto you the whole armour of God, that ye may be able to withstand in the evil day, and having done all, to stand.

Ephesians 6:13

All I Need

Heavenly Father, You are a God of hope, joy, and great love. I don't need signs or wonders. I often wait for people or situations to turn from hopeless to hopeful. But my hope is in You. I need not wait for anything else or look for some other source. I quiet myself before You this morning and ask that You renew the hope within my heart. Thank You, Father. Amen.

What more could anyone ask for than to be a child of the living God? We have the promise of abundant life and the hope of eternal life in heaven!

And now, Lord, what wait I for? my hope is in thee.
PSALM 39:7

DAY 236

Sanctified by Christ

Jesus, sanctify my life. Let the Holy Spirit burn out the sin and flesh that tarnish me and make me unfit for the kingdom. Do a whole work in me, spirit, soul, and body. Without Your sanctification, I tend to be earthly minded and give in to fleshly desires. Set me apart from the world by purifying my life and making me ready for Your return. Amen.

Only Christ can sanctify us. Allow His Spirit to do His work in you, spirit, soul, and body.

And the very God of peace sanctify you wholly; and I pray God your whole spirit and soul and body be preserved blameless unto the coming of our Lord Jesus Christ.

1 THESSALONIANS 5:23

The Hope of Heaven

God, I cannot even imagine heaven. But I know it will be a glorious place. I know that there will be no more tears there. You tell me that in Your Word. Even the sweetest worship of my God that I take part in on this earth is nothing like the worship there. Constantly, we will worship You, Father! You have prepared a place for me there. What hope I have in You. Amen.

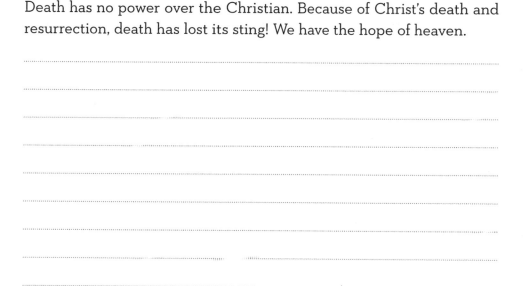

Death has no power over the Christian. Because of Christ's death and resurrection, death has lost its sting! We have the hope of heaven.

In my Father's house are many mansions: if it were not so, I would have told you. I go to prepare a place for you.

JOHN 14:2

Prove All Things

Jesus, help me not to accept something just because it's popular or trending or someone I admire says it's right. Help me to prove out what is being said or done to see if it's from You or You approve of it. Show me that which is from You, that which is good for me, and help me to hold fast to those things approved by You. Amen.

❧

Don't accept anything that isn't backed up by scripture. If it contradicts God's Word, leave it alone. Run from it.

_____

_____

_____

_____

_____

_____

_____

_____

_____

_____

Prove all things; hold fast that which is good.

1 Thessalonians 5:21

The Return of Jesus Christ

Jesus, I know that You will return. I find great hope in the scriptures that give a preview of that day! We don't know everything about it. We certainly cannot predict the timing of it. But the Bible assures us that You are coming back! This world is temporal. It shall all pass away one day. I am so thankful that I know beyond a shadow of a doubt that my Savior is coming back. Amen.

The Bible says that as lightning that comes from the east is visible in the west, so shall the second coming of Christ be! He is coming again.

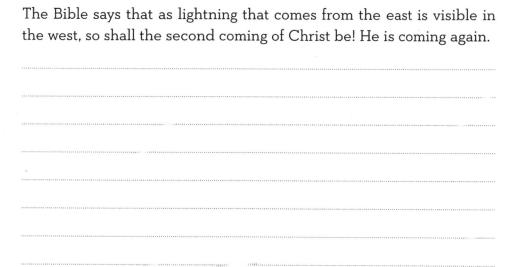

And then shall they see the Son of man coming in the clouds with great power and glory. And then shall he send his angels, and shall gather together his elect from the four winds, from the uttermost part of the earth to the uttermost part of heaven.

MARK 13:26–27

Faithful to the End

God, keep me faithful to the end of the race. In spite of what others say or think about me, don't let me waver. When You told Noah to build an ark, he didn't waver from that responsibility. He kept working on the commission You gave him until it was finished. He must have endured criticism and ridicule every day, but still he persisted. Give me that same kind of persistence. Amen.

Faithfulness is of utmost importance to God. He's looking for faithful people. Do you qualify?

_____

_____

_____

_____

_____

_____

_____

_____

_____

_____

_____

And Noah did according unto all that the Lord commanded him.

GENESIS 7:5

Love in Deed and Truth

Father, it is easy to say the words "I love you," but it is harder to live them. You want Your children to love their enemies. You tell us to love through action and with truth. These are high callings that require Your Holy Spirit working in us. Use me as a vessel of love today in my little corner of the world. Let me love through my deeds and not just with words. Amen.

Saying "I love you" should mean something. *Love* is a powerful word. Be sure that your actions back up the saying when you use it.

My little children, let us not love in word, neither in tongue; but in deed and in truth.

1 JOHN 3:18

Trusting God

God, You made Sarah and Abraham a promise that they would have a son in their old age. The Bible says Sarah laughed because she and her husband were both too old to have children. Nevertheless, they took You at Your word and believed the promise. Help me to take You at Your word and never doubt when You make a promise. Help me to be as trusting as Sarah was, knowing that with man this thing was impossible, but with You, it would happen. Amen.

Never doubt what God tells you He will do. He always keeps His promises. He cannot lie.

_____

_____

_____

_____

_____

_____

_____

_____

Is any thing too hard for the LORD? At the time appointed I will return unto thee, according to the time of life, and Sarah shall have a son.

GENESIS 18:14

Love Covers Sins

Lord, all of my sin was nailed to the cross when Your Son died for me. Without grace, I am but filthy rags before a holy God. But through Christ, I am adopted as Your daughter, forgiven. There is pride in this daughter, God. Pride that resists forgiveness. Pride that says, "I am right." Remind me of the multitude of my own sins that Your love covered through Jesus. Help me to love others well. Amen.

Unforgiveness rarely hurts the other person as much as it hurts the one who refuses to forgive. Love is at the heart of forgiveness.

Hatred stirreth up strifes: but love covereth all sins.

PROVERBS 10:12

My Light and My Salvation

Lord, when I needed a savior, You were my salvation. When the days are dark, You are my light. When I'm afraid, You're my strength, providing the courage I need. With You at my side, why should I be afraid of anything? But I'm human, and sometimes I am. Instill in me this promise that David recorded that You are the strength of my life and I don't have to be afraid. Amen.

When you're afraid, remember that the Lord is your strength. You're not in the battle alone.

The LORD is my light and my salvation; whom shall I fear?
the LORD is the strength of my life; of whom shall I be afraid?
PSALM 27:1

The Love of a True Friend

God, I am thankful for friends in my life who are more like family. They accept me as I am, and yet they help me to grow. When times are bad, they are there. They stick it out with me. They call. They show up. They listen. They encourage. Friends like this are few and far between. Thank You, Father, for friends who love at all times. Make me such a friend as well. Amen.

Do you have a friend in need? Find a way today to bless that friend. Instead of asking what you can do, just do something. It will mean so much.

....

....

....

....

....

....

....

....

....

....

....

A friend loveth at all times, and a brother is born for adversity.

PROVERBS 17:17

He Lights the Way

God, when Moses led the children of Israel out of Egypt, You went before them. They didn't have to guess which direction to take. A pillar of a cloud by day and a pillar of a fire by night let them know You were present. I don't have to guess which direction to take either. If I listen to Your Spirit, You will guide me every step I take. Thank You for Your direction, Lord. Amen.

Instead of guessing which direction to take in life, pray and ask God where He would have you go. He's better than any compass, map, or navigation system. He won't lead you wrong.

....

....

....

....

....

....

....

....

And the LORD went before them by day in a pillar of a cloud, to lead them the way; and by night in a pillar of fire, to give them light; to go by day and night: he took not away the pillar of the cloud by day, nor the pillar of fire by night, from before the people.

EXODUS 13:21–22

Better Than Life

I praise You, Father, for who You are! Your loving-kindness exceeds that of any human. You are good. You are beautiful. You are all things right and true. In You and through You, all things take their shape. This world is Your creation, and You choose to keep the Earth turning on its axis. You bless us when we do not deserve blessing. Your love is better than life! Amen.

Consider your greatest desires. Think of all the dreams you have for your future. God is greater than anything else. Keep Him central in your life.

Because thy lovingkindness is better than life, my lips shall praise thee.

PSALM 63:3

God Gives What's Needed

Father, I want to do whatever You ask of me, but sometimes I get anxious, nervous, and wonder what I was thinking when I agreed to it. But I don't have to worry about how to do something You ask me to do. You're concerned about every detail. I know You will give me the strength, ability, and knowledge to carry out the task You have for me. All I have to do is trust You. Amen.

God is in the details of your life. Anything He asks of you, He will come alongside and help you accomplish the task. He won't leave you helpless.

And Moses said unto the children of Israel, See, the LORD hath called by name Bezaleel the son of Uri, the son of Hur, of the tribe of Judah; and he hath filled him with the spirit of God, in wisdom, in understanding, and in knowledge, and in all manner of workmanship.

EXODUS 35:30–31

Showing That I Love God

How do I show that I love You, God? It must be more than merely a phrase I use in prayer. The way I show it is to keep Your commandments. I need Your strength for this. I fail every day. Renew my desire to live according to Your principles. They are not suggestions. They are commands. Honoring them will cause me to see You at work in my life. I love You, Lord. Amen.

Do you know God's commandments for your life? They are in His Word. We have access to them in scripture. God desires that we keep the commands He has given.

He that hath my commandments, and keepeth them, he it is that loveth me: and he that loveth me shall be loved of my Father, and I will love him, and will manifest myself to him.

JOHN 14:21

God Is Merciful

Father, I'm feeling overwhelmed by situations that are out of my control. These things fill me with stress and sometimes fear. Extend Your hand of mercy to me. I trust You to take care of me. Hide me in the shadow of Your wings, and keep me safe from all the outside forces that seem bent on defeating me. Thank You for being my refuge. Amen.

Are you facing something that has you stressed and fearful? Fall on the mercies of God. He is your refuge in times of trouble.

Be merciful unto me, O God, be merciful unto me: for my soul trusteth in thee: yea, in the shadow of thy wings will I make my refuge, until these calamities be overpast.

PSALM 57:1

All of Me

When You were asked what the greatest commandment was, You did not evade the question. You answered clearly, Jesus. I am to love the Lord my God with all of my heart, soul, mind, and strength. I am to love my God with all of me. There should be nothing left over when I am finished loving God. No crumbs I feed to the idols that crave my attention. It is all for You. Amen.

Where do you spend most of your time? Your money? Your attention? Are you loving the Lord your God with all of your heart, soul, mind, and strength?

_____

_____

_____

_____

_____

_____

_____

_____

And Jesus answered him, The first of all the commandments is, Hear, O Israel; The Lord our God is one Lord: and thou shalt love the Lord thy God with all thy heart, and with all thy soul, and with all thy mind, and with all thy strength: this is the first commandment.

MARK 12:29–30

Honoring God

Father, I hear so many people taking Your name in vain. I see it on social media and hear it on television. Do they not know it's wrong, or do they not care? I think some expressions have become so common people don't even realize what they're saying. Lord, let me always be offended by the misuse of Your name. Help me never to use it in a disrespectful way. Amen.

Are you aware of your everyday speech? Does it glorify God, or do you use expressions that bring dishonor to Him? Ask God to show you anything that might be disrespectful of Him.

Thou shalt not take the name of the LORD thy God in vain: for the LORD will not hold him guiltless that taketh his name in vain.

DEUTERONOMY 5:11

Loving My Neighbors

Jesus, You did not stop with the first commandment. The second is strong as well. You tell me to love my neighbor. But You don't stop there. You tell me to love my neighbor as myself. But my neighbors are not always easy to love! Still, this is Your command. You have given me Your Holy Spirit. May I love with Your Spirit, for my own is lacking. Amen.

Consider who your neighbors are. They are not just the people who live on either side of your home. Your neighbors include all the people in your life. Love them well.

_____

_____

_____

_____

_____

_____

_____

_____

And the second is like, namely this, Thou shalt love thy neighbour as thyself. There is none other commandment greater than these.

MARK 12:31

He'll Bring You Out

God, I know You're always working for my good. The children of Israel were in Egyptian bondage for many years and suffered greatly. But You brought them out so You could give them an inheritance promised to their fathers. You had to bring them out to bring them in. Sometimes, You have to bring me through a situation to bring me into the blessings You have for me. Thank You for working for my good. Amen.

You may wonder why life is carrying you down the hard road you're traveling. Remember that God is in control and He will bring you out at His appointed time.

And the LORD shewed signs and wonders, great and sore, upon Egypt, upon Pharaoh, and upon all his household, before our eyes: and he brought us out from thence, that he might bring us in, to give us the land which he sware unto our fathers.

DEUTERONOMY 6:22–23

Only One Master

Father, there are so many things in this world that fight for my affection. It seems there is always a new product or style that the advertisements say I can't live without! It is easy to get caught up in materialism. Guard my heart, Father, and guard even my tongue. Remind me that the word love should not be used loosely. I love You, Father. Be Lord of my life, I pray. Amen.

Do you catch yourself uttering "I love. . ." statements about the latest fashions or a yummy dessert? Consider the power of those words. Perhaps reserve them for things that really matter.

_____

_____

_____

_____

_____

_____

_____

_____

No man can serve two masters: for either he will hate the one, and love the other; or else he will hold to the one, and despise the other. Ye cannot serve God and mammon.

MATTHEW 6:24

Choose Life

Father, sometimes I make the wrong choices. Forgive me. My heart's desire is to please You, and I know Your desire is to bless me, but You allow me to make the choices. Give me wisdom in the choices I make. Help me to choose life that I might experience Your blessings. Amen.

What choices are you facing today? God allows us to make our own choices, but the consequences are ours to bear if we make the wrong choice. Choose life in God.

....

....

....

....

....

....

....

....

....

....

....

I call heaven and earth to record this day against you, that I have set before you life and death, blessing and cursing: therefore choose life, that both thou and thy seed may live.

DEUTERONOMY 30:19

DAY 257
Love Is of God

God, how will others know that I am a Christian? They will know it by my love. As I go through this day, give me opportunities to express love. It may be through a kind word of encouragement, an act of kindness, or even just a smile. Put the people in my path and on my heart today that need to experience Your love through me. Use me as a vessel of Your love. Amen.

The words of an old song put it this way: "And they'll know we are Christians by our love, by our love. Yes, they'll know we are Christians by our love."

_____

_____

_____

_____

_____

_____

_____

_____

Beloved, let us love one another: for love is of God; and every one that loveth is born of God, and knoweth God.

1 John 4:7

Put Confidence in God

Father, the harlot Rahab took a chance that the spies who came to search out her homeland would do her the favor of saving her and her family. She was aware that You were God in their lives. She put her confidence in their God. As a result, she and her family were saved alive when Israel invaded Jericho. I have confidence in You because You're faithful and You are my God. Amen.

What have you placed your confidence in? Are you relying on people, possessions, or social status? These things will let you down. Confidence in God always pays off.

_____

_____

_____

_____

_____

_____

_____

_____

And as soon as we had heard these things, our hearts did melt, neither did there remain any more courage in any man, because of you: for the LORD your God, he is God in heaven above, and in earth beneath.

JOSHUA 2:11

A Thankful Heart

Lord, everything good in my life comes from You. Often I forget to thank You. I am thankful for Your provision and Your protection. I am thankful for my family and friends. I am most of all thankful for the joy of my salvation, which comes through Christ. Give me a grateful heart, I pray. Let me always remember that every good and perfect gift comes from Your hand. Amen.

A thankful heart will take you a long way in life. Try writing down three things you are thankful for at the start or close of each day.

And let the peace of God rule in your hearts, to the which also ye are called in one body; and be ye thankful.

COLOSSIANS 3:15

Take Heed unto Yourselves

*Lord, sometimes I see evil people committing horrendous crimes,
and fear tries to rise up within me. Your Word promises that we don't
have to be afraid when we trust You. Make Yourself known to me in
a greater way. Wipe away the fingers of fear that try to choke me.
I know You will fight for those who belong to You. Thank You
for being with me every day. Amen.*

Does the evening news strike fear in your heart sometimes? Does the
enemy try to take away your confidence in God? Remember that God
has promised to fight for you.

*One man of you shall chase a thousand: for the LORD your God,
he it is that fighteth for you, as he hath promised you.*

JOSHUA 23:10

Blessing for Resisting Temptation

Father, help me to resist temptation today. Every day I am tempted to sin in different ways. As I am still before You this morning, ready my heart and mind for battle. I am a warrior in this world. I know that in Your strength, I can overcome the temptations I face. Thank You for the promise that You will bless me with the crown of life. I love You, Lord. Amen.

Don't try to resist temptation on your own. When you are tempted to sin, remember to take every thought captive to Christ.

....

....

....

....

....

....

....

....

....

Blessed is the man that endureth temptation: for when he is tried, he shall receive the crown of life, which the Lord hath promised to them that love him.

JAMES 1:12

God in You

Father, when You called Gideon a mighty man of valor and challenged him to go to battle, he didn't have a lot of confidence in himself. He called himself the least in his father's house. I've been guilty of feeling that same way, thinking that there must be someone else who was better for the job than me. Thank You for showing me that it's not who I am but who You are that gets the job done. Amen.

Don't allow self-esteem to get in the way of God's work. Without Him, we can do nothing, but God in us can accomplish great things.

....

....

....

....

....

....

....

....

And he said unto him, Oh my Lord, wherewith shall I save Israel? behold, my family is poor in Manasseh, and I am the least in my father's house. And the LORD said unto him, Surely I will be with thee, and thou shalt smite the Midianites as one man.

JUDGES 6:15–16

Blessing Others

Words of blessing and encouragement from other believers mean so much to me. Help me, Lord, to be generous in my blessings to those whom You have placed within my circle of influence. Often, I pray for friends and family members privately, but I know how much it means to me when a blessing is spoken in my presence. Help me to bless others and to encourage them along their journeys. Amen.

When someone presents you with a problem, ask if you might pray right then! The Bible tells us that where two or more gather in His name, there He is also.

The LORD bless thee, and keep thee: the LORD make his face shine upon thee, and be gracious unto thee: the LORD lift up his countenance upon thee, and give thee peace.
NUMBERS 6:24–26

DAY 264

Praise Is Comely

Lord, let praise to You be on my lips every day. I don't want it to be something I feel obligated to do. It should be a spontaneous fountain bubbling up inside of me for all You mean to me and all You've done. Praise sounds so much better coming out of my mouth than grumbling and complaining. Help me to rejoice in You. Amen.

It's better for us and those around us if we start off each day with praise to the Lord. Grumbling and complaining makes us frown. A smile on our face looks so much better than a frown.

Rejoice in the LORD, O ye righteous:
for praise is comely for the upright.
PSALM 33:1

I will bless the LORD at all times:
his praise shall continually be in my mouth.
PSALM 34:1

Blessing for Walking with God

Give me strength, Father, to stand up for what I believe in and not just go along with the crowd. While I am in the world, as a Christian I am certainly not of it. I must guard my heart and walk in Your ways. Protect me from those who would attempt to lead me astray, I ask. Even if it means that I must endure persecution, I will walk with You, God. Amen.

Those who are closest in your life will have great influence on you. You will be blessed if you choose to walk in the counsel of the godly rather than the ungodly.

Blessed is the man that walketh not in the counsel of the ungodly, nor standeth in the way of sinners, nor sitteth in the seat of the scornful.

PSALM 1:1

To Obey Is Better

Lord, forgive me when I choose my own will and ignore Yours or try to make Your will fit mine. Help me to set aside my own agenda, even when it looks and sounds good, and do what You want done. Guide me in the right direction. I know it sounds foolish, but sometimes I think I know best. That's a lie from the enemy. You always know what's best for me. Help me to be obedient to You and submissive to Your will. Amen.

It's never a good idea to let your own agenda get in the way of what God is speaking to you about. He always knows best, and He requires obedience on our part.

And Samuel said, Hath the LORD as great delight in burnt offerings and sacrifices, as in obeying the voice of the LORD? Behold, to obey is better than sacrifice, and to hearken than the fat of rams.

1 SAMUEL 15:22

Blessed for Keeping God's Word

Hearing and doing are two separate things. I see this when I watch a two-year-old child at play. He hears his mother say no to something that may harm him but turns and attempts the act anyway. I do this with You sometimes, don't I, God? I read Your Word and understand it, but I go my own way. I try it alone. Help me to hear Your Word. . .and keep it. Amen.

To truly digest scripture, you must read it and spend time meditating on it. Set aside time each day to spend in God's Word.

But he said, Yea rather, blessed are they that hear the word of God, and keep it.

LUKE 11:28

My Brother's Keeper

*Lord, help me to be aware of other people and their needs.
Show me how to be my brother's keeper. Sometimes I get so wrapped
up in what's going on in my world that I forget to come alongside my
brothers and sisters in the Lord and lend them my help and support.
Help me to show them compassion as You would do. Amen.*

The world says it's all about "me," but according to God's Word, that's not true. While there is a time for us to take care of our own problems, we need to be supportive of those around us. We need to be our brother's and sister's keeper.

*And the LORD said unto Cain, Where is Abel thy brother?
And he said, I know not: Am I my brother's keeper?*

GENESIS 4:9

Blessed in Mourning

Jesus, You spoke to the people on the hillside that day. How I wish I could have seen and heard You. But I have in the Bible a record of what You said. You said that I will be comforted in times of mourning. You called me blessed. Sometimes I feel that no one understands the deep loss I have experienced. Thank You for this promise. It shows me how much You care. Amen.

In just nine statements regarding blessing in His Sermon on the Mount, Christ found it important to address those who mourn. He cares about your grief.

Blessed are they that mourn: for they shall be comforted.
MATTHEW 5:4

Chosen by God

*Father, thank You for choosing to send Your Son to die for me,
and thank You for choosing to bless me with the precious gift
of salvation. Jesus made the way for us to be reconciled to You.
It's so comforting to be able to approach You in prayer anytime
I want to and to know that I'm welcome in Your presence. Amen.*

You were chosen by God to receive the wonderful gift of salvation and be
able to approach Him whenever you need to. Visit the throne room today.

*Blessed is the man whom thou choosest, and causest to approach
unto thee, that he may dwell in thy courts: we shall be satisfied
with the goodness of thy house, even of thy holy temple.*

PSALM 65:4

Hungering and Thirsting for Righteousness

Father, even as I hunger and thirst for righteousness, sometimes I am distracted. Sometimes I only halfheartedly seek You. But I do long to live as You wish for me to live. I know that through Christ, You see me as righteous. Help me to deeply desire to resist sin and to know You and glorify You fully in this life. I know that blessing comes with this type of pursuit of holiness. Amen.

Seek Christ daily. Seek Him with your whole heart. A real, intimate, growing relationship with Him will lead you to right living and right choices.

Blessed are they which do hunger and thirst after righteousness: for they shall be filled.

MATTHEW 5:6

He Will Preserve You

Lord, thank You for watching over me today. I don't know what's in store for me, but Your Word has promised me that You will preserve my coming in and going out. Not just today, but from now on. I can go about my tasks knowing that You are with me, watching what goes on around me, preserving me. Amen.

God has His eye on you. You can go through your day knowing that He is with you, preserving you and keeping you.

_____

_____

_____

_____

_____

_____

_____

_____

_____

_____

The LORD shall preserve thy going out and thy coming in from this time forth, and even for evermore.

PSALM 121:8

Blessed for Persecution

Father, I have never known real persecution. I have not been thrown into prison or had my life threatened for proclaiming Christ. But there are times when others don't understand my choices. They think I am being old-fashioned. It hurts. Thank You for declaring a blessing over me when I take a stand in Your name. If I am ever truly persecuted for my faith in Christ, give me strength to withstand it. Amen.

It is okay if people do not understand or respect the choices that you make based on God's Word. God will bless you when you take a stand.

Blessed are ye, when men shall revile you, and persecute you, and shall say all manner of evil against you falsely, for my sake.
MATTHEW 5:11

Justified by Faith

Jesus, thank You for making the supreme sacrifice for me. I needed a savior. I needed to be redeemed. I couldn't do anything to save myself. There were no laws, traditions, or works that could redeem me. But faith in You brought about the salvation that I needed so badly. What a wonderful gift from You. Amen.

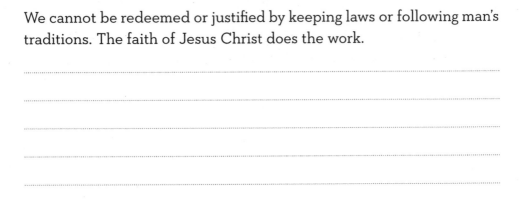

We cannot be redeemed or justified by keeping laws or following man's traditions. The faith of Jesus Christ does the work.

....

....

....

....

....

....

....

....

....

....

....

....

Knowing that a man is not justified by the works of the law, but by the faith of Jesus Christ, even we have believed in Jesus Christ, that we might be justified by the faith of Christ, and not by the works of the law: for by the works of the law shall no flesh be justified.

GALATIANS 2:16

Blessing Those Who Hurt You

God, when someone hurts me, I don't feel like blessing him or her. Remind me what Your Word teaches about love. Love keeps no record of wrongs. Love forgives. It restores. Love tries again. Love lets it go. Love blesses even when it's not my turn to bless! Give me a spirit of love that trumps evil. And allow me to bless those who hurt me. I can only do so in Your power. Amen.

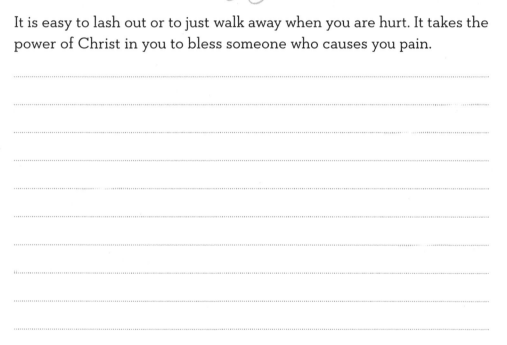

It is easy to lash out or to just walk away when you are hurt. It takes the power of Christ in you to bless someone who causes you pain.

Not rendering evil for evil, or railing for railing: but contrariwise blessing; knowing that ye are thereunto called, that ye should inherit a blessing.

1 PETER 3:9

Liberty in Christ

*Jesus, thank You for the liberty that has made me a free person in You.
Help me to live a godly life and not look back at those things You
have freed me from. Show me how to stand fast in this liberty
so that I won't get tangled up in the world and be
under bondage to Satan again. Amen.*

If Christ has set you free, determine in your heart to live for Him, and
don't allow yourself to get involved in worldly pursuits.

_____

_____

_____

_____

_____

_____

_____

_____

_____

_____

*Stand fast therefore in the liberty wherewith Christ hath made us free,
and be not entangled again with the yoke of bondage.*

GALATIANS 5:1

A Blessed Memory

Heavenly Father, I want to live my life in a manner that honors You.
When I come to the end of this life, I want my memory to be blessed.
May those I leave behind be led closer to You because they knew me.
I pray that You will help me to have an eternal view each day
and help me to be a woman of character and grace. Amen.

How will you be remembered? You can impact the world for Christ or you can live for yourself. You can encourage others or discourage them.

The memory of the just is blessed: but the name of the wicked shall rot.
PROVERBS 10:7

Fruit of the Spirit

Lord, help me to produce fruit in my life. You've told us in Your Word what kind we should bear. It's a list I can't produce in myself. Without the Holy Spirit, I can't show love, exhibit joy, or have peace. I can't be long-suffering with others, have gentleness, goodness, or faith without You. I won't be meek or have temperance in my life unless I'm walking with You. Cause me to be a fruit producer. Amen.

Those who are led by the Spirit produce fruit that is pleasing to God.

But the fruit of the Spirit is love, joy, peace, longsuffering, gentleness, goodness, faith, meekness, temperance: against such there is no law.

GALATIANS 5:22–23

Bless His Name

Jesus, You alone are worthy of all of my praise. I bless Your name. One day I will worship You with no end, no holding back, and no earthly distraction. I will worship You in heaven forever and ever. . . with the angels and with all of Your people. For today, I go into Your world, and I will choose to bless Your name in the present. Accept my offering of praise. Amen.

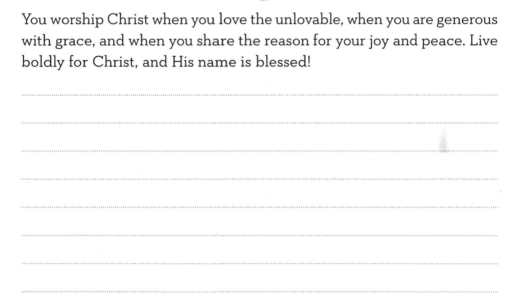

You worship Christ when you love the unlovable, when you are generous with grace, and when you share the reason for your joy and peace. Live boldly for Christ, and His name is blessed!

_____

_____

_____

_____

_____

_____

And I beheld, and I heard the voice of many angels round about the throne and the beasts and the elders: and the number of them was ten thousand times ten thousand, and thousands of thousands; saying with a loud voice, Worthy is the Lamb that was slain to receive power, and riches, and wisdom, and strength, and honour, and glory, and blessing.

REVELATION 5:11-12

Bearing Others' Burdens

Father, sometimes my burdens get heavy and I'm consumed by what I have to do. Your Word tells us we are to bear other people's burdens too. Some days, I don't feel I can do that. Strengthen me to be obedient to Your Word. Help me not to be self-centered, thinking only of myself. Help me to be a burden bearer for those around me. Amen.

Thinking of others and sharing their burdens can help take our minds off ourselves.

Bear ye one another's burdens, and so fulfil the law of Christ.
GALATIANS 6:2

Trust in God

*Heavenly Father, Your ways and Your Word are perfect and true.
I trust in You, God. You are my shield and Protector. I read and
memorize Your Word so that in times of trouble, it will come to mind.
There is such power in Your Word. I will stand for what is right.
I trust in You to take care of me all the days of my life. Amen.*

Where have you placed your trust? Most things in this life will pass away, but the Word of the Lord will stand forever. Place your trust in the eternal God, your Creator.

*As for God, his way is perfect; the word of the LORD is tried:
he is a buckler to all them that trust in him.*

2 SAMUEL 22:31

Strong in the Lord

Jesus, some days I feel like a spiritual weakling. It seems everything gets to me. I'm stressed and out of sorts with others. I grumble or whine, maybe not out loud, but in my mind. That's not how You want us to be. You want us to be strong. I can't do it by myself. I'm so thankful I have You walking with me to make me strong through Your power and might. Amen.

You don't have to fight this battle all alone. You can be strong in Christ by His power and might.

....

....

....

....

....

....

....

....

....

Finally, my brethren, be strong in the Lord, and in the power of his might. Put on the whole armour of God, that ye may be able to stand against the wiles of the devil.

EPHESIANS 6:10–11

Above All Things

Father, I must resist the urge to put my trust in anything that is of this world. I will trust in the name of the Lord, my God. I don't need a fancy car or house. It doesn't matter if I have a lot of friends or just a few. I will place my trust in You, and You will see me through in this life. I love You, Lord. Thank You for being trustworthy. Amen.

On April 15, 1911, the "unsinkable" *Titanic*—carrying only enough lifeboats to save approximately half of its passengers—collided with an iceberg and sank in the North Atlantic Ocean. Surely no one at the time thought that would happen! Be sure that your foundation is Christ Jesus.

Some trust in chariots, and some in horses: but we will remember the name of the LORD our God.

PSALM 20:7

Save Me, O God

God, some days I feel like Peter, who decided he could walk on water and then began to sink when he stepped out into the sea. When trouble is all around me, I feel like I'm sinking into deep water. It's then that I can cry out to You, "Save me, O God." What would I do if I didn't know You? The answer is simple. I would drown. Thank You for reaching out and saving me. Amen.

When you feel yourself sinking into deep waters, cry out to God. He has a rescue plan.

Save me, O God; for the waters are come in unto my soul. I sink in deep mire, where there is no standing: I am come into deep waters, where the floods overflow me.

PSALM 69:1–2

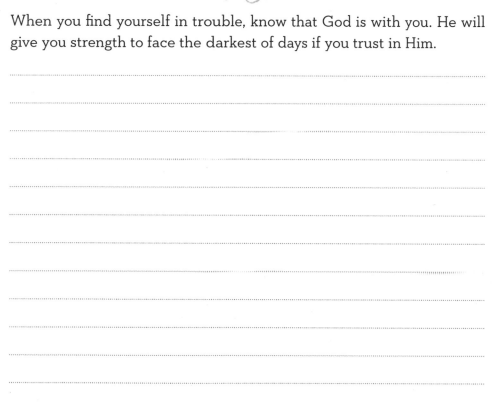

DAY 285

God Knows

Father, You are always watching over us. You are aware of all things.
You know Your children by name. I love the scripture that says You
know the number of hairs on my head. And because You know me
so well, Lord, You see that I trust in You. I will not fear trouble,
for You will be my stronghold when it comes. Amen.

When you find yourself in trouble, know that God is with you. He will
give you strength to face the darkest of days if you trust in Him.

_____

_____

_____

_____

_____

_____

_____

_____

_____

_____

The LORD is good, a strong hold in the day of trouble;
and he knoweth them that trust in him.

NAHUM 1:7

Conversation in Heaven

Jesus, I know You hear all I say, and yet sometimes I don't think before I speak. I say foolish things. I give my opinion without thinking who it might hurt. I pass judgment because I think I'm right when I may very well be wrong. Cause me to stop and think before uttering words that aren't necessary or edifying. Help me to remember that my conversation isn't hidden; it's in heaven. Amen.

Every time we open our mouths, our words are heard in heaven.

For our conversation is in heaven; from whence also we look for the Saviour, the Lord Jesus Christ.

PHILIPPIANS 3:20

Trustworthy through the Ages

Lord, so many have come before me that have trusted in Your name.
I read about the heroes and heroines of the Bible. They were ordinary
men and women whom You used in extraordinary ways. Noah trusted
You when You told him to build an ark. Abraham trusted You when
You asked him to sacrifice his beloved son, Isaac. You have proven
Yourself trustworthy. Teach me to trust You more. Amen.

Ask an older Christian to tell you about a time that God delivered him
or her. He has been faithful to His children through the ages. You can
trust Him!

Our fathers trusted in thee: they trusted, and thou didst deliver them.

PSALM 22:4

Be Content

God, why do we think we need all these extra things to live? Is it really necessary to drive around in an expensive car or buy all the trinkets we see in the stores? Do I really need to wear designer labels? All these things are nice and You've blessed us with more than enough, but they're not necessary to life. Help me to learn contentment. When I have You, I have all I need. Amen.

Everywhere we look, we're bombarded with the latest trends and gadgets. Our senses are teased into thinking we have to have the newest items to be in step with everyone else. What we really need is God's direction on how to be content with what we have.

Not that I speak in respect of want: for I have learned, in whatsoever state I am, therewith to be content.

PHILIPPIANS 4:11

A Testimony

*My life is a song of praise to You, my faithful Father, the Giver of life!
When people hear my testimony of Your goodness, may they come
to know You. I want others to notice the difference in me and wonder
why I have such joy, such peace. May I point them to You, Lord,
and may they trust in You for salvation. You are the
Way, the Truth, and the Life. Amen.*

Does your life look and sound like a praise song to the Father? Are you
a reflection of His love to those around you?

*And he hath put a new song in my mouth, even praise unto our God:
many shall see it, and fear, and shall trust in the LORD.*

PSALM 40:3

Be On Guard

Jesus, keep me on guard against the lure of the world and its philosophies. Don't let me be deceived by anyone no matter who they are. Sometimes ideas and thoughts sound good, but they're really false beliefs covered in just enough truth to fool someone. Help me to follow You and stand on Your Word in all situations. Amen.

Study the Bible for yourself. Know what it says, and don't receive anything that contradicts God's Word.

Beware lest any man spoil you through philosophy and vain deceit, after the tradition of men, after the rudiments of the world, and not after Christ. For in him dwelleth all the fulness of the Godhead bodily.

COLOSSIANS 2:8–9

DAY 291

Trust in His Strength

Lord, at times I get cocky. I step out on my own and think I've got everything under control. But then something happens that shakes my world. I find myself calling on You and hoping You will come. You always show up. You always remember me. I am Your child. Help me to trust You before I am desperate. Help me to remember the source of my strength. Amen.

Be careful where you place your trust. It is only through Christ that we are truly strong.

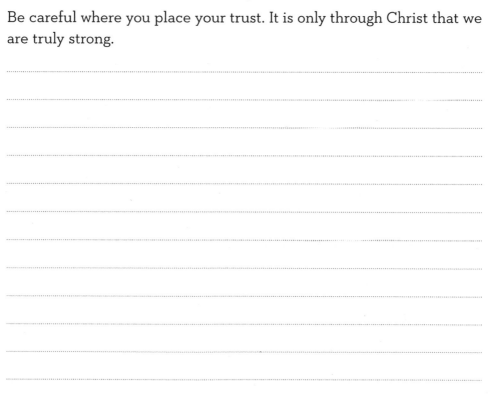

For I will not trust in my bow, neither shall my sword save me.

PSALM 44:6

Put Off Sin

God, sometimes people think of sin as something big like theft and murder, but Your Word teaches that there are many things we need to get rid of if we call ourselves Christians. The world doesn't consider anger, lying, or bad language as sin, but the apostle Paul told the Colossian church that they needed to put off these things also and put on the new man in Christ. Help me to put off sin and put on Christ. Amen.

As Christians we need to live according to God's Word, not like the world around us. Christ has made us a new person.

But now ye also put off all these; anger, wrath, malice, blasphemy, filthy communication out of your mouth. Lie not one to another, seeing that ye have put off the old man with his deeds; and have put on the new man, which is renewed in knowledge after the image of him that created him.

Colossians 3:8–10

A Leader Who Trusts in God

Hezekiah was not a perfect king, Father. But he was known as a leader who trusted You. That is how I want to be known. As I live out my life on this earth, please use me as an example of one who trusts in You. This is what I want to be known for in the end. It makes all the difference in the world. Amen.

A true believer who trusts in God stands out from the crowd. Consider those whom you lead. Do they know that your trust is in the Lord?

_____

_____

_____

_____

_____

_____

_____

_____

He trusted in the LORD God of Israel; so that after him was none like him among all the kings of Judah, nor any that were before him. For he clave to the LORD, and departed not from following him, but kept his commandments, which the LORD commanded Moses.

2 KINGS 18:5–6

Don't Be Envious

Father, the psalmist Asaph writes that he was envious when he saw the prosperity of the wicked. He said they weren't in trouble like other men; they have more than they could wish for. But then he went into the sanctuary of God and realized how foolish he was. The wicked would perish, but he had God to hold his hand. Lord, help me not to envy the wicked, but draw me close to You. You are the strength of my heart and my portion forever. Amen.

When you compare the blessings of God to the prosperity of the world, God always wins out. Eternal riches far outweigh earthly riches. Read Psalm 73 to hear what Asaph said about it.

....

....

....

....

....

....

....

For I was envious at the foolish, when I saw the prosperity of the wicked. . . . Until I went into the sanctuary of God; then understood I their end. . . . But it is good for me to draw near to God: I have put my trust in the Lord GOD, that I may declare all thy works.

PSALM 73:3, 17, 28

In Tough Times

Lord, I will trust You on the hardest days. When trials and tribulations come my way, I tend to doubt Your presence and Your goodness. Things can seem to spin out of control. I look up and wonder where You are in it all. But You are there. You are my God, worthy of my trust. And the trials strengthen me. They bring about patience, and patience leads to experience, and experience to hope. Amen.

Job chose to trust in the Lord regardless of external circumstances. We must decide in the light that we will trust Him in the darkness.

....

....

....

....

....

....

....

....

....

....

....

Though he slay me, yet will I trust in him.

JOB 13:15

Called for a Purpose

Lord, I know You called me for a purpose. Contrary to what I think sometimes, I'm not here to just enjoy life and have a good time. You paid a great price to redeem me. Your Word says I've been called with a holy calling according to Your purpose and grace. Show me how to live for Your purpose and not my own. Amen.

God has called you for a purpose. What are you living for today?

_____

_____

_____

_____

_____

_____

_____

_____

_____

_____

Who hath saved us, and called us with an holy calling, not according to our works, but according to his own purpose and grace, which was given us in Christ Jesus before the world began.

2 TIMOTHY 1:9

Trust in His Guidance

Father, this morning I come before You and I praise You. You are good and loving. You have only my very best interest at heart. Take my hand and lead me. Show me the way to go. Like a child being carried in a loving parent's arms, let me relax and trust You. I know that You will never lead me astray. Thank You, God, for this assurance. Amen.

God will walk with you all the days of your life. Trust Him to lead you. He wants to make the crooked paths straight before His children.

Cause me to hear thy lovingkindness in the morning; for in thee do I trust: cause me to know the way wherein I should walk; for I lift up my soul unto thee.

PSALM 143:8

Sound Words

Lord, help me to know the difference between sound words and those that are not from You. Let me cling to what Your Word teaches me and those who preach the Gospel according to Your truth. Help me to also teach and speak sound words to others for Your glory. Amen.

❧

Cling to the sound words you've been taught according to God's Word. Don't be drawn away by some new teaching that sounds good unless it's based on the Bible.

Hold fast the form of sound words, which thou hast heard of me, in faith and love which is in Christ Jesus.

2 TIMOTHY 1:13

More Blessed to Give

Jesus, You are the ultimate Giver. You gave up Your life on the cross. Help me to give on a daily basis, not just on special occasions. Give me eyes to see people in need, whether they are in need of material blessings or simply my time. Make me a generous giver of all that You have entrusted to me. May my resources and talents flow freely rather than stagnating as I hoard them. Amen.

It is better to give than to receive. Practice extravagant giving. Give more than your excess. Give of your very best. It will always come back to you.

I have shewed you all things, how that so labouring ye ought to support the weak, and to remember the words of the Lord Jesus, how he said, It is more blessed to give than to receive.

ACTS 20:35

Showing Meekness

Father, there are some who get involved in worldly matters and use it as a reason for doing things that are displeasing to You. Help me to stand for what I believe, but never at the expense of my relationship with You. We must not take a job, run for an office, or get involved in public demonstrations and use these things as a reason to hurt others. Let the Holy Spirit show me what to get involved in and what to avoid. Amen.

As Christians, we must act in a way that shows Christ to the world whether we're a public servant or just a good citizen.

_____

_____

_____

_____

_____

_____

_____

_____

Put them in mind to be subject to principalities and powers, to obey magistrates, to be ready to every good work, to speak evil of no man, to be no brawlers, but gentle, shewing all meekness unto all men.

TITUS 3:1–2

Giving in Jesus' Name

There are so many ways to proclaim Your name, Jesus. One of them is through giving. Make my heart merciful toward those in need. Remind me that while I feel I cannot change the world, I can make a difference. Your Word points out that even the smallest gesture of kindness counts. Even when You see me offer a drink of water to one person in need, You are pleased. Show me opportunities to serve. Amen.

The story of the Good Samaritan in the Bible is powerful. As Christ followers, we should not be passersby but participants in meeting the needs of the poor.

....

....

....

....

....

....

....

....

And whosoever shall give to drink unto one of these little ones a cup of cold water only in the name of a disciple, verily I say unto you, he shall in no wise lose his reward.
MATTHEW 10:42

Live Godly

Jesus, I know You will return soon for Your believers. Your Word tells us that there is also judgment coming upon the earth. I want to be ready for Your return. Show me how to live godly—what kind of person I need to be in light of Your soon return. I want to conduct myself in such a way that I will be ready at all times to meet You. Amen.

We need to live in such a way that we will be an example of godliness to others and be ready to meet Christ when He returns.

_____

_____

_____

_____

_____

_____

_____

_____

_____

_____

_____

_____

Seeing then that all these things shall be dissolved, what manner of persons ought ye to be in all holy conversation and godliness.

2 PETER 3:11

A Cheerful Giver

It is a privilege to give to Your kingdom, heavenly Father.
Whether I am writing out my tithe check or giving of my time and
talents on a mission trip, let me give with joy. I have learned that
You provide. I cannot "out give" my God! You are too loving,
too generous, too great! Regardless of my circumstances,
mold my heart that I might always give with cheerfulness. Amen.

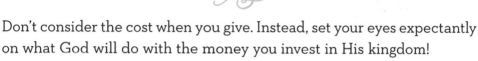

Don't consider the cost when you give. Instead, set your eyes expectantly
on what God will do with the money you invest in His kingdom!

Every man according as he purposeth in his heart, so let him give;
not grudgingly, or of necessity: for God loveth a cheerful giver.

2 CORINTHIANS 9:7

Confess and Pray

*Father, sometimes I have a hard time confessing my faults. I guess
I have too much pride. I don't want anyone to know my faults.
Forgive me. You told us to confess and pray for one another that
we could be healed. I need this healing, and I want others to receive it
too. Help me to confess my faults and pray for others when
they confess. Extend healing to each of us. Amen.*

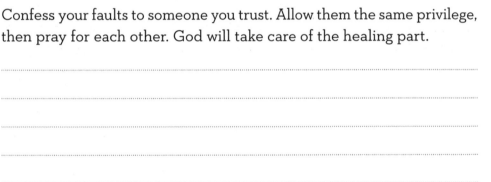

Confess your faults to someone you trust. Allow them the same privilege,
then pray for each other. God will take care of the healing part.

*Confess your faults one to another, and pray one for another,
that ye may be healed. The effectual fervent prayer
of a righteous man availeth much.*

JAMES 5:16

Tithing

Father, You tell me to test You with my tithe. If I give it generously, You will bless my household. I will find it overflowing with blessing. There will not be enough room to contain all of it. I imagine the windows of heaven opening and blessings just pouring, pouring, pouring down on me! You are not a God who sprinkles blessings or gives them in little pinches or samples. You are an extravagant Giver. Amen.

If you have become comfortable with giving a tenth of all your income, test God further. Give even more. There is incredible blessing to be found in giving to the Lord.

_____

_____

_____

_____

_____

_____

_____

Bring ye all the tithes into the storehouse, that there may be meat in mine house, and prove me now herewith, saith the LORD of hosts, if I will not open you the windows of heaven, and pour you out a blessing, that there shall not be room enough to receive it.

MALACHI 3:10

Don't Be Troubled

Lord, it's easy to tell someone else not to be troubled, but it's difficult when I face something that troubles me. Lord, keep my mind focused on You so my heart doesn't become troubled with all that's happening around me. I believe Your promises, and I know You will give me peace. Amen.

Jesus told us not to be troubled. We can trust Him and His Word. Ask Him for peace in your heart, your mind, and your home.

Let not your heart be troubled: ye believe in God, believe also in me.

JOHN 14:1

Giving as I Am Able

Father, Your commands are just and good. You do not demand that the poor give large sums of money that are impossible for them to attain. You ask that we give as we are able. So many times, I could give more. Show me when and how much to give. Help me to give as I am able, for that is what You expect of me, Lord. Nothing more, but certainly. . .nothing less. Amen.

Even in times when money is short, trust the Lord and give to Him. He will bless you for remaining faithful in your tithing.

_____

_____

_____

_____

_____

_____

_____

_____

_____

Every man shall give as he is able, according to the blessing of the LORD thy God which he hath given thee.
DEUTERONOMY 16:17

This Same Jesus

Jesus, I wasn't alive while You were here on earth. I didn't experience an actual physical walk with You like the disciples did, but I'm walking by faith now and believing that You will return. Your Word says in Acts 1:11 that the same Jesus that ascended will return for us. I'm waiting expectantly to see You, Lord. Even so, come, Lord Jesus. Amen.

The same Jesus that was resurrected and ascended to the Father is coming back for you and me.

....

....

....

....

....

....

....

....

And while they looked stedfastly toward heaven as he went up, behold, two men stood by them in white apparel; which also said, Ye men of Galilee, why stand ye gazing up into heaven? this same Jesus, which is taken up from you into heaven, shall so come in like manner as ye have seen him go into heaven.

ACTS 1:10–11

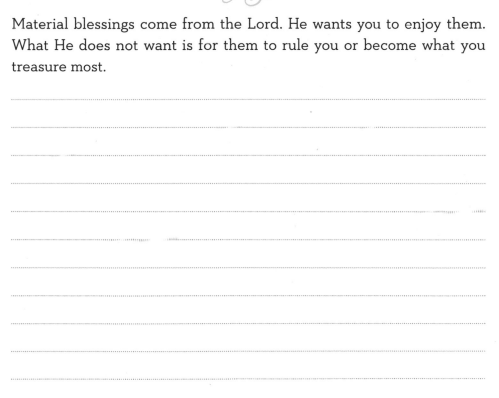

DAY 309

Where Is My Treasure?

God, You have blessed me with good things. I treasure my family and friends. I find happiness in decorating my home and hosting parties. My job is a big part of my identity. I enjoy shopping and putting together a new outfit. It feels good to get a compliment occasionally! But where is my treasure? If these things begin to take priority over You, I know that my heart is in the wrong place. Amen.

Material blessings come from the Lord. He wants you to enjoy them. What He does not want is for them to rule you or become what you treasure most.

For where your treasure is, there will your heart be also.

MATTHEW 6:21

God Thinks about You

Father, I'm so glad You think about me, that You have plans for me, that You know all about me and still love me. I'm sure there are other people who think about me and their thoughts aren't good or peaceful. Thank You for making plans for me and caring about what comes my way. I'm glad You are taking care of everything on my behalf right up until the end. Amen.

No matter how bad things may seem, God has a plan for you, and His thoughts for you are of peace and not evil.

For I know the thoughts that I think toward you, saith the LORD, thoughts of peace, and not of evil, to give you an expected end.
JEREMIAH 29:11

The Ultimate Gift

God, You gave the ultimate gift. You gave us Your only Son whom You loved so much. I can't imagine how it must have felt to watch Him go from heaven's glory to a manger bed in a lowly stable in Bethlehem. And yet, You gave Him to us freely. Out of Your great, great love for us, You sent Your Son into the world. Thank You for the gift of salvation through Jesus. Amen.

Is there someone in your life that does not know Jesus as his or her Savior? Share Christ with that person. Tell your friend about the gift of Jesus.

....

....

....

....

....

....

....

....

....

*For God so loved the world, that he gave his only begotten
Son, that whosoever believeth in him should not
perish, but have everlasting life.*

JOHN 3:16

Be Ready

*Jesus, I don't know when You're coming, but I know You are.
People have tried to predict when You will return. Some people have
even named a certain date, but they don't know. Only Your Father
knows that day and time. It's going to happen when we least expect
it. I just want to be ready no matter when that time comes.
Help me to keep my mind on You and Your return. Amen.*

Live as if Jesus were coming today, because He could come at any time
and we don't want to miss it.

---

*Therefore be ye also ready: for in such an hour
as ye think not the Son of man cometh.*

MATTHEW 24:44

A Legacy of Generosity

Father, the psalmist declares that he has never seen the righteous forsaken or his children going hungry. This inspires me. I know that You bless those who give. I want to leave a legacy of generosity for my children or for others that are influenced by my life. What they see me practicing regarding giving will impact their choices. May we be a generous family, always looking for opportunities to show mercy. Amen.

Whether you know it or not, others are watching the way that you give. Are you merciful, always looking for ways to bless those around you?

_____

_____

_____

_____

_____

_____

_____

_____

I have been young, and now am old; yet have I not seen the righteous forsaken, nor his seed begging bread. He is ever merciful, and lendeth; and his seed is blessed.

PSALM 37:25–26

Light of the Body

Lord, Matthew tells us that the light of the body is the eye and it can be good or evil. Help me to be careful what I focus my eyes on. I need to choose carefully what I watch, read, or observe. If I choose the wrong things, I'll see darkness, but if I'm focusing on You and Your will for me, I will have light in my life. Cause me to choose carefully what I see with my eyes. Amen.

Be careful what you choose to look at; it could bring you darkness.

The light of the body is the eye: if therefore thine eye be single, thy whole body shall be full of light. But if thine eye be evil, thy whole body shall be full of darkness. If therefore the light that is in thee be darkness, how great is that darkness!

MATTHEW 6:22–23

A Soft Heart

Shutting my hand is the same as hardening my heart. What a powerful warning! Father, I want to have a soft heart, one that is moved to give and to bless others. Protect me from greed that so easily could cause me to tighten my grip on my wallet. To whom You have given much, much is expected. You expect me to give freely. Help me to be a good steward of Your blessings. Amen.

Would you rather err on the side of giving to someone whose need is not as great as he portrays or on the side of selfishness and greed?

....

....

....

....

....

....

....

....

If there be among you a poor man of one of thy brethren within any of thy gates in thy land which the LORD thy God giveth thee, thou shalt not harden thine heart, nor shut thine hand from thy poor brother: but thou shalt open thine hand wide unto him, and shalt surely lend him sufficient for his need, in that which he wanteth.

DEUTERONOMY 15:7–8

DAY 316

Cease to Do Evil

God, I can't wash away my own sin, but the blood of Your Son, Jesus, can make me clean when I do sin. Thank You for the gift of cleansing that You have provided. There are things I can do. I can stop doing, thinking, or speaking evil. I can spend time doing for others. I can commit to doing things that please You. Help me to choose to do the right thing at all times. Amen.

God has provided a way for us to be clean. It's up to us to receive His gift and give up the bad habits we've cultivated in our lives.

....
....
....
....
....
....
....
....
....
....

Wash you, make you clean; put away the evil of your doings from before mine eyes; cease to do evil; learn to do well; seek judgment, relieve the oppressed, judge the fatherless, plead for the widow.

ISAIAH 1:16–17

It All Belongs to God

Lord, everything I have is Yours. The whole earth was created by You. You are the Giver of all good things, and the Bible says that You will never withhold any good gift from Your children. Lord, let me remember that it all belongs to You. I am just a manager of some of Your resources. May I use the gifts You have given me to glorify You. In Jesus' name, I pray, amen.

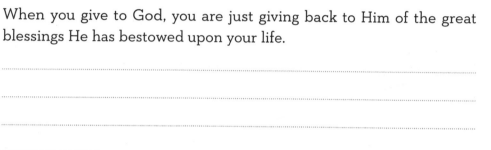

When you give to God, you are just giving back to Him of the great blessings He has bestowed upon your life.

And all the tithe of the land, whether of the seed of the land, or of the fruit of the tree, is the LORD's: it is holy unto the LORD.
LEVITICUS 27:30

Willing and Obedient

Lord, sometimes I'm not too willing to do what You want me to do. My own will gets in the way. There have been times when I've been disobedient. I confess this to You now. Please forgive me. If I choose to be a willing and obedient servant, good things are in store for me. Give me a willing heart, and help me to choose obedience to You over my own will. Amen.

Why is it so hard for us to choose to be willing and obedient when we know God has good things in store for us? It doesn't make sense for us to choose bad things over good. Choose good today.

_____

_____

_____

_____

_____

_____

_____

_____

_____

If ye be willing and obedient, ye shall eat the good of the land.

ISAIAH 1:19

The Heart of Giving

Jesus, You see the heart of the giver. I can imagine the shock of the disciples when You declared the widow's small gift greater than that of the rich. They gave of their excess. She gave all she had. She wanted to be part of the kingdom work. She trusted You to meet her needs. May I have a true giver's heart. May I give sacrificially as the widow did that day. Amen.

If you are not giving until it hurts, until you notice a bit of a lower bank account balance, you may not be giving enough. Give beyond the pocket change. Give sacrificially.

....

....

....

....

....

....

And there came a certain poor widow, and she threw in two mites, which make a farthing. And he called unto him his disciples, and saith unto them, Verily I say unto you, That this poor widow hath cast more in, than all they which have cast into the treasury: for all they did cast in of their abundance; but she of her want did cast in all that she had, even all her living.

MARK 12:42–44

Watching Daily

God, I want to know more about You. I want a closer relationship with You. I know that means I need to give up spending so much time doing what I want and seek You more. I need to listen more attentively for Your voice. I need to search Your Word, looking for direction and instruction to live a godly life. Help me to seek a more intimate relationship with You. Amen.

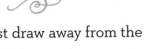

To draw closer to God, we must draw away from the world and our will.

_____

_____

_____

_____

_____

_____

_____

_____

_____

_____

_____

*Blessed is the man that heareth me, watching daily
at my gates, waiting at the posts of my doors.*
PROVERBS 8:34

A Woman Who Fears the Lord

God, I want to be a Proverbs 31 woman. My focus should not be on external beauty or the clothing and jewelry that I wear. Rather, may others notice my heart that is forever seeking You. I want nothing more than to be known as a woman of God. Protect me from vanity. Outward beauty is not lasting, but a beautiful spirit is. I meditate upon Your Word now, Lord. I want to honor You. Amen.

Pretty clothes and makeup are not wrong in and of themselves. But remember that these things are not where your true beauty lies.

Favour is deceitful, and beauty is vain: but a woman that feareth the LORD, she shall be praised.

PROVERBS 31:30

DAY 322

A Generous Soul

Father, give me a generous soul and spirit. Help me to reach out to those who cross my path today. Show me the needs of others that I might minister to them. Someday I might be the one in need of a helping hand, but whether I am or not, help me to be like You. You served others, even those who weren't considered worthy of Your help. Let me be Your hand extended. Amen.

People who cross our paths are there for a reason. We need to find out what that reason is.

The liberal soul shall be made fat: and he that watereth shall be watered also himself.

<small>PROVERBS 11:25</small>

DAY 323

The Beauty of the Lord

*May my pursuit of You, Lord, be my "one thing." May I praise You
and serve You in this life, which is but training camp for eternity!
I look forward to heaven, Father, where I may truly know the depths
of Your beauty. I see glimpses of Your beauty in Your creation.
One day it will be fully revealed. What a glorious day that will
be! Until then, be my "one thing." I love You, Lord. Amen.*

You are not a servant in your Father's house nor a traveler passing through
who stays a night or two. You are a daughter of the King, and you may
dwell with Him always!

*One thing have I desired of the LORD, that will I seek after; that I may
dwell in the house of the LORD all the days of my life, to behold the
beauty of the LORD, and to enquire in his temple.*

PSALM 27:4

Building My House

Father, help me to be a good builder of my own home. Help me to speak kind words to my family even on those days when I'm tired or stressed. Cause me to be kind even when others aren't kind to me. Show me how to keep peace under my roof. Help me to build the kind of home that others want to dwell in and where Your presence is felt by all. Amen.

The way we build our home determines what kind of life we're going to live day by day. It's important that we follow God's blueprint as we build.

....
....
....
....
....
....
....
....
....

Every wise woman buildeth her house:
but the foolish plucketh it down with her hands.
PROVERBS 14:1

Beauty in Age

As I grow older, Father, grant me the wisdom to see that there is beauty in age as well as in youth. You give young men strength, and certainly that is needed. They must work hard and protect their families. Some even serve in the military. But You give old men wisdom. Their gray hairs were earned through lessons learned and trials conquered. Grant me strength, and mature me as I age, I pray. Amen.

Seek wise and godly counsel when you encounter trials. Christian men and women who are older than you are a great source of wisdom.

The glory of young men is their strength: and the beauty of old men is the grey head.

PROVERBS 20:29

Praying for Others

God, I've never suffered like Job did, but I have had people hurt me. When Job prayed for his friends who had spoken harsh things to him, You delivered him and blessed him. Help me to be willing to pray for those who treat me wrong whether they acknowledge their wrong or not. In return, I can receive deliverance and blessing from You. Amen.

When we harbor resentment and hurt against others, we end up the loser. Pray for those who have wronged you so you can receive deliverance and blessing from God.

....

....

....

....

....

....

....

....

....

....

And the LORD turned the captivity of Job, when he prayed for his friends: also the LORD gave Job twice as much as he had before.

JOB 42:10

Beautiful Feet

Oh Lord, I imagine Your smile when You see Your people taking the Gospel of Christ into the world. Whether it is in a village on the other side of the world or right here in my neighborhood or office, may I have beautiful feet! May I carry the Gospel of Christ to others. I will run with the message, for it is life changing! How beautiful are the feet of those who bring good news. Amen.

May we feel a sense of urgency to share the Gospel with the lost. All of heaven rejoices when just one soul is saved!

How beautiful upon the mountains are the feet of him that bringeth good tidings, that publisheth peace; that bringeth good tidings of good, that publisheth salvation; that saith unto Zion, Thy God reigneth!

ISAIAH 52:7

Perfect Peace

Father, I love the perfect peace that You give, but there are times when I don't have that peace. It's not Your fault; it's totally mine. You will keep us in perfect peace if our mind is stayed on You. That's where the problem lies. Sometimes I allow my mind to get so muddled with life that it strays from You. Please keep me on track. I want that perfect peace in my life. Amen.

When life gets in the way and you're not experiencing perfect peace, check the location of your mind.

....

....

....

....

....

....

....

....

....

....

....

Thou wilt keep him in perfect peace, whose mind is stayed on thee: because he trusteth in thee.

ISAIAH 26:3

A Meek and Quiet Spirit

*God, in Your economy a meek and quiet spirit is worth more than gold.
It is not corruptible. It is eternal. Give me such a spirit. Make me into
a better listener, I pray. Set a guard over my tongue at times when
I should not speak. Teach me to walk humbly with You, Father,
and to serve people in Your name. A gracious, godly spirit
is what You desire to see in me. Amen.*

You can have a quiet spirit regardless of your personality type. God
desires a kind sweetness in you as His daughter.

*Whose adorning let it not be that outward adorning of plaiting the
hair, and of wearing of gold, or of putting on of apparel; but let it
be the hidden man of the heart, in that which is not corruptible,
even the ornament of a meek and quiet spirit, which is
in the sight of God of great price.*

1 PETER 3:3–4

Establish Your Heart

Lord, I'm not always a patient person, but I want to be where it concerns my relationship with You. I know You're coming soon. I want to be established in You. I want to stay faithful until Your return. Establish my heart so there is no room for anything except Your will in my life. If I'm in Your will, I know everything else that pertains to me will fall into place. Amen.

We need to wait patiently and be established in Christ so we will be ready for His return.

Be ye also patient; stablish your hearts: for the coming of the Lord draweth nigh.

JAMES 5:8

DAY 331
Radiance

May my countenance reflect that I am a believer, Father! May people know just by the joy in my eyes that I am a Christ follower. Peace and joy are commodities of the Christian that should show in their faces. I want to have such a radiance, Lord. May I never be ashamed of You. May I be proud to give an answer for my joy. It comes from the King of kings! Amen.

We are to be salt and light, seasoning and illuminating. We are to shine for the Lord in this world. Is your face radiant with the joy of the Lord?

They looked unto him, and were lightened: and their faces were not ashamed.

PSALM 34:5

Great Is Our Lord

God, You are so amazing. I really can't put into words just how awesome You are. I praise You this morning for Your greatness. The stars hang in place every night, twinkling out their light. You've even named them and can call them by name. You know the number of the hairs on my head. You breathed life into us. You are worthy of all honor, power, and glory. Amen.

Take time to look around at the magnificence of our God. Spend some time thinking about all He does for you every day. He is worthy of your praise.

He telleth the number of the stars; he calleth them all by their names. Great is our Lord, and of great power: his understanding is infinite.

PSALM 147:4–5

Beauty for Ashes

Loving God, You alone are able to give beauty for ashes. You replace mourning with joy. Use me, in spite of the disappointments and losses I have experienced. Today is a new day. I want to be a tree of righteousness that bears good fruit, fruit that glorifies You and leads others into Your saving presence. Replace my depression with contentment and my sorrow with praise. This is my prayer today, in Jesus' name. Amen.

In your deepest sorrow, there is still hope. In your greatest loss, God can provide a way for survival. He declares that you are more than a conqueror through Christ.

_____

_____

_____

_____

_____

_____

_____

To appoint unto them that mourn in Zion, to give unto them beauty for ashes, the oil of joy for mourning, the garment of praise for the spirit of heaviness; that they might be called trees of righteousness, the planting of the LORD, that he might be glorified.

Isaiah 61:3

DAY 334

Wisdom in Your Heart

God, I need wisdom and knowledge to guide me in my daily life. I need to learn discretion and have understanding. I know the presence of these will keep me from trouble. Teach me how to receive these things so I can live a life pleasing to You and make a good life for myself and those around me. Amen.

When we ask God for wisdom and knowledge, learn discretion, and have understanding, we can rest assured He will bless us and we in turn will be a blessing to others.

When wisdom entereth into thine heart, and knowledge is pleasant unto thy soul; discretion shall preserve thee, understanding shall keep thee.

PROVERBS 2:10–11

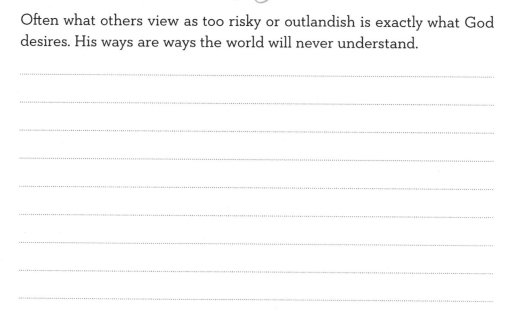

DAY 335

A Beautiful Work

Lord, I read of the woman who poured out a flask of expensive perfume upon Your feet. The disciples did not understand, but You saw it as a beautiful work. Give me a heart like hers. Whatever I possess, whatever comes my way, help me to fling it all forth for Your glory. Let me use it wisely but extravagantly to honor my King. I love You, Lord. Make my life a beautiful work for You. Amen.

Often what others view as too risky or outlandish is exactly what God desires. His ways are ways the world will never understand.

But when his disciples saw it, they had indignation, saying, To what purpose is this waste? For this ointment might have been sold for much, and given to the poor. When Jesus understood it, he said unto them, Why trouble ye the woman? for she hath wrought a good work upon me.

MATTHEW 26:8–10

A Song in the Night

Father, thank You for giving me a song in the night. Sometimes when I awaken during those hours, the darkness is overwhelming. The enemy tries to speak fear into my heart. How sweet it is when You bring a song to my mind. When I start to hum that song or go through the words in my mind, the darkness begins to lift. Before I know it, sweet peace has arrived and I can sleep once again. Amen.

Ask God to give you a song in the night for those times when the darkness crowds in.

_____

_____

_____

_____

_____

_____

_____

_____

_____

_____

I call to remembrance my song in the night: I commune with mine own heart: and my spirit made diligent search.

PSALM 77:6

Don't Toot Your Own Horn

Lord, help me not to boast and toot my own horn when I accomplish things. I know that it's only through You that I have been able to achieve anything. Because of Your grace and blessing, I can do something to glorify You. Help me to give You glory for all that I do. Promotion comes through You, not anything I do. Amen.

It's been said that you can accomplish much if you don't care who gets the credit for it. Choose to give God the credit in your life.

Lift not up your horn on high: speak not with a stiff neck. For promotion cometh neither from the east, nor from the west, nor from the south. But God is the judge: he putteth down one, and setteth up another.

PSALM 75:5–7

DAY 338
Our Comforter

Jesus, thank You for sending us another Comforter, the Holy Spirit, who is an agent of change and power in my life. He does so much for me every day. When I'm troubled and don't know how to deal with the problem, I can go to prayer and the Holy Spirit will intercede for me as I seek You. When I need comfort, He's there for me. When the enemy comes in, the Holy Spirit empowers me to have victory. Amen.

The Holy Spirit works in our lives to give us those things we need to be overcomers.

Likewise the Spirit also helpeth our infirmities: for we know not what we should pray for as we ought: but the Spirit itself maketh intercession for us with groanings which cannot be uttered.
ROMANS 8:26

Washed, Sanctified, Justified

Jesus, I'm so thankful for Your work on the cross. Without Your sacrifice, I would be lost like those in the world. I would be no better than a thief, idolater, or murderer. But I've been washed in Your precious blood, sanctified by Your Spirit, and justified in Your name. What a work of redemption You've done on me. Thank You. Amen.

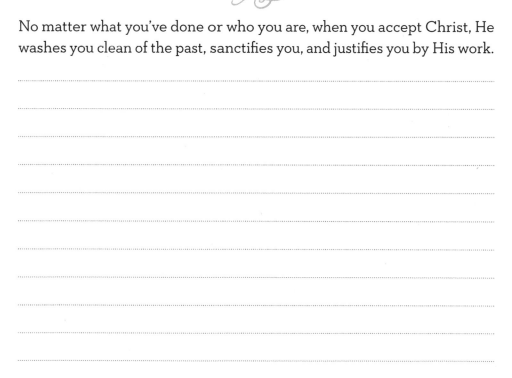

No matter what you've done or who you are, when you accept Christ, He washes you clean of the past, sanctifies you, and justifies you by His work.

And such were some of you: but ye are washed, but ye are sanctified, but ye are justified in the name of the Lord Jesus, and by the Spirit of our God.

1 Corinthians 6:11

Unite My Heart

Father, sometimes I feel like I'm working against myself. I struggle at times to overcome the flesh and its desires. Teach me how to walk in Your truth, not mine. Unite my heart with Yours so I will not give in to temptation or walk afar off. If there's unity between my heart and Yours, I can walk in a way that pleases You and brings glory to Your name. Amen.

Does your heart go off on its own path sometimes? Ask God to unite your heart with His so you can stay on the right road.

. . . .

. . . .

. . . .

. . . .

. . . .

. . . .

. . . .

. . . .

. . . .

. . . .

Teach me thy way, O LORD; I will walk in thy truth: unite my heart to fear thy name.

PSALM 86:11

Perfecting Holiness

*God, cleanse me from fleshly desires that separate me from You.
Sanctify me by Your Word as I read and study it each day. As Your
Spirit reveals sin to me, help me to repent and turn away from the
wrong. Show me how to live a holy life before You and others. Let the
fire of the Holy Spirit burn away everything that keeps me from
having holiness in my life. Make me holy as You are holy. Amen.*

Sometimes the things that prevent us from living a holy life seem harmless. Allow the fire of the Holy Spirit to burn away anything that keeps you from being perfected in holiness.

*Having therefore these promises, dearly beloved, let us cleanse
ourselves from all filthiness of the flesh and spirit,
perfecting holiness in the fear of God.*

2 Corinthians 7:1

The Secret Place

God, I want to dwell in Your secret place where Your shadow will cover and protect me. In Your secret place, I know I'll find rest for my weary soul. I'll find peace from the stress of daily life. I'll find strength to face tomorrow. Help me to discover this place in You and make it my permanent home. Amen.

Living under the shadow of the Almighty ensures that we are living where the devil can't defeat us.

....

....

....

....

....

....

....

....

....

He that dwelleth in the secret place of the most High shall abide under the shadow of the Almighty. I will say of the LORD, He is my refuge and my fortress: my God; in him will I trust.

PSALM 91:1–2

His Mercy Endures

Father, thank You for Your enduring mercy. I'm in need of it every day even though I don't deserve it. Without Your mercy, how could I make it? When I fail, Your mercy endures. You don't give up on me although You certainly have the right. You continue to love me and give me what I need for each day. When I make the same mistakes over and over, Your mercy is still there. Thank You for mercy. Amen.

Mercy has rewritten many lives. When you feel like a total failure, remember that God has enduring mercy to keep you going.

Praise ye the LORD. O give thanks unto the LORD;
for he is good: for his mercy endureth for ever.
PSALM 106:1

DAY 344
Able to Keep

Lord, I'm thankful this morning that I know You. I can trust You with all my secrets. I don't have to be afraid You will betray me. People may do or say something to betray me, but You never will. You are able to keep those things that I've committed unto You, and I have confidence that You will keep them for me forever. Amen.

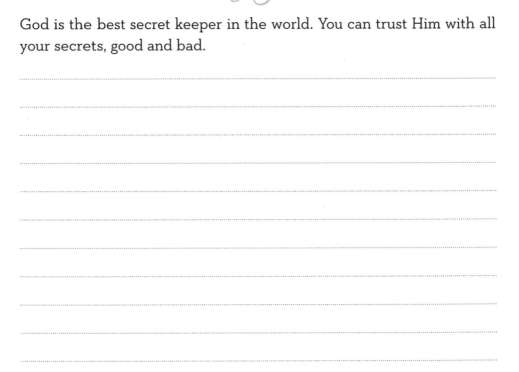

God is the best secret keeper in the world. You can trust Him with all your secrets, good and bad.

For the which cause I also suffer these things: nevertheless I am not ashamed: for I know whom I have believed, and am persuaded that he is able to keep that which I have committed unto him against that day.
2 TIMOTHY 1:12

Perilous Times

*God, when I watch the news, I know we are living in the perilous times that Paul spoke to Timothy about. I can read through the list and see all these things happening in our world. It's a fearful time, but I know Your children don't have to be afraid. We are kept by Your power and are anxiously awaiting Your return.
Thank You for that assurance. Amen.*

God is able to keep those who belong to Him. Hold His hand as the world crashes around you. He will never let go of you.

*This know also, that in the last days perilous times shall come. . . .
Yea, and all that will live godly in Christ Jesus shall suffer
persecution. . . . But continue thou in the things which
thou hast learned and hast been assured of,
knowing of whom thou hast learned them.*

2 TIMOTHY 3:1, 12, 14

DAY 346
Keep the Faith

Jesus, Paul suffered many things to spread the Gospel, but he didn't give up. He stayed on course and he finished the race. He knew there was a crown waiting for him. He fought to the very end. Give me that same determination. Help me to fight a good fight and finish the course. Increase my faith, and help me to keep that faith until my work is finished. Amen.

No matter what obstacles the devil throws in your path, never give up. Keep the faith; finish the race. There's a reward waiting for you.

I have fought a good fight, I have finished my course, I have kept the faith: henceforth there is laid up for me a crown of righteousness, which the Lord, the righteous judge, shall give me at that day: and not to me only, but unto all them also that love his appearing.

2 TIMOTHY 4:7–8

Praise His Name

*God, I praise Your name this morning. Since the beginning of time,
You have shown Yourself worthy of praise. You have given me life
and loved me when I was unlovable. Help me to have a praise on
my lips for You at all times. When I get up in the morning,
let me praise Your name. Before I go to sleep at night,
may there be praise for You on my lips. Amen.*

God is worthy of our praise from the time we get up until we go to bed
at night. Give Him the praise He is due.

_____

_____

_____

_____

_____

_____

_____

_____

*Praise ye the LORD. Praise, O ye servants of the LORD, praise the
name of the LORD. Blessed be the name of the LORD from this time
forth and for evermore. From the rising of the sun unto the going
down of the same the LORD's name is to be praised.*

PSALM 113:1–3

DAY 348
Don't Boast of Tomorrow

Father, I know that all things are in Your hands. You are in control of my days and my time. I don't know what's going to happen tomorrow, but You do. Help me not to boast about what I'm going to do or be in the days to come but instead trust You to order my days. I don't know what I may face, but You're holding my hand and I'm trusting You to guide me. Amen.

You may not know what tomorrow holds, but you can know who holds your hand. Make sure you never let go of God's hand.

_____

_____

_____

_____

_____

_____

_____

_____

_____

Boast not thyself of to morrow; for thou knowest not what a day may bring forth.
PROVERBS 27:1

DAY 349
His Word in My Heart

God, help me to hide Your Word in my heart. Saturate me in Your Word so that I'm thinking about it all through the day. Let it become as natural to me as breathing. Knowing Your Word keeps me on the right track. Hiding it in my heart keeps me from going astray. Your Word teaches, convicts, and assures me. Let it become so much a part of me that I wear it like a garment. Amen.

When we become saturated in God's Word, we know how to live for Him. It will instruct our days and keep us during times of temptation.

....

....

....

....

....

....

....

....

With my whole heart have I sought thee: O let me not wander from thy commandments. Thy word have I hid in mine heart, that I might not sin against thee.
PSALM 119:10–11

Daily Needs

Jesus, I'm so thankful You care about our daily needs. When the multitudes followed You, You were concerned that they had nothing to eat. You provided for them. You've provided for me and my family numerous times. It's so comforting to know I serve a Savior who cares whether I have anything to eat, a place to sleep, or something to wear. Thank You, Jesus, for caring about Your children and meeting their needs. Amen.

Jesus is concerned about your daily needs. If you need something, feel free to ask Him. He cares for you.

_____

_____

_____

_____

_____

_____

_____

_____

In those days the multitude being very great, and having nothing to eat, Jesus called his disciples unto him, and saith unto them, I have compassion on the multitude, because they have now been with me three days, and have nothing to eat.

MARK 8:1–2

Resurrection Life

Jesus, when Lazarus died, You spoke encouraging words to his sister Martha. You told her that You are the resurrection and the life. I'm so glad that those same words are for me today. Because of You, I have life and hope. Because of the resurrection, I live, not just here on earth, but with You throughout eternity. Because of You, I shall never die. Thank You for that promise and the hope I have in You. Amen.

We don't have to fear death—because Jesus has been there before us, and we live because He lives.

Jesus said unto her, I am the resurrection, and the life: he that believeth in me, though he were dead, yet shall he live: and whosoever liveth and believeth in me shall never die. Believest thou this?

JOHN 11:25–26

Power to Speak

Jesus, thank You for sending the Holy Ghost to us. You promised that He would be a Comforter that would be with us to empower us to be witnesses. I need that power to speak to others words that will lead them to You. Without the power of the Holy Ghost and His guidance, our efforts are fruitless. He can take our words and make them profitable for Your kingdom. Amen.

Your efforts may seem small, but the Holy Ghost can magnify them for God's purposes.

But ye shall receive power, after that the Holy Ghost is come upon you: and ye shall be witnesses unto me both in Jerusalem, and in all Judaea, and in Samaria, and unto the uttermost part of the earth.

ACTS 1:8

Your Own Business

Lord, forgive me for sometimes being a busybody and sticking my nose in other people's business. I tell myself it's because I'm concerned about the other person, and sometimes that's true. Other times, I'm just being nosy. Help me to be quiet and do my own business and let everyone else take care of theirs. Amen.

Contrary to what we think, we don't need to know what everyone else is doing. We don't always want others to know what we're doing, so we should grant them the same courtesy.

And that ye study to be quiet, and to do your own business, and to work with your own hands, as we commanded you; that ye may walk honestly toward them that are without, and that ye may have lack of nothing.

1 Thessalonians 4:11–12

Abstain from Evil

Lord, I know evil sometimes shows up as a wolf in sheep's clothing. It doesn't look harmful or evil. It's all white and emits a soft baa so that we won't know what it really is. Give me knowledge and wisdom to recognize that there's a wolf underneath that seemingly harmless cover. Other times, the appearance of evil is faint or maybe just hinted at. Help me to abstain from the very appearance or hint of evil. Amen.

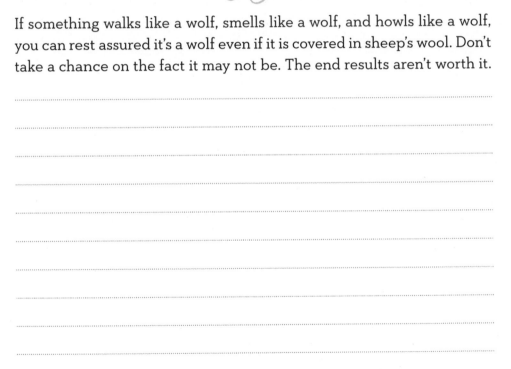

If something walks like a wolf, smells like a wolf, and howls like a wolf, you can rest assured it's a wolf even if it is covered in sheep's wool. Don't take a chance on the fact it may not be. The end results aren't worth it.

Prove all things; hold fast that which is good.
Abstain from all appearance of evil.
1 THESSALONIANS 5:21–22

Think upon His Name

Father, as I go through my day, help me to think about You and Your goodness. Give me opportunities to speak to others about the blessings You have given me. There are those who are sad, needy, and without hope. They need to hear of Your goodness. Help me to speak often with others who know You that we might glorify Your name together. Help me to think upon Your name today. Amen.

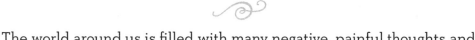

The world around us is filled with many negative, painful thoughts and events. We can dwell on these things and let it bring us down, or we can think upon the name of our God and be encouraged.

Then they that feared the LORD spake often one to another: and the LORD hearkened, and heard it, and a book of remembrance was written before him for them that feared the LORD, and that thought upon his name.

MALACHI 3:16

House of the Lord

God, I'm so thankful for the right to worship as I want to. It's such an honor and privilege to go to Your house and worship with the rest of the saints. It's a great blessing to experience Your presence as we lift our hearts in worship. King David knew that same feeling. He was glad to go into Your house. Thank You for a place to worship You with people of like-minded faith. Amen.

Going to God's house is like finding an oasis in the desert. It's a place to find refreshing for soul, spirit, and body.

_____

_____

_____

_____

_____

_____

_____

_____

_____

I was glad when they said unto me, Let us go into the house of the LORD. . . . Because of the house of the LORD our God I will seek thy good.

PSALM 122:1, 9

Vain Labor

Lord, forgive me for those times when I've tried to build or do things on my own. It's useless. Not only do I make mistakes, but the quality of the work falls short. It's useless to try to build something without Your direction. Without You, we're fumbling around, trying to make sense of our work. Help us to rely upon You and follow Your plans for our work. Amen.

Follow God's blueprint for building your relationship with Him. You will have a sturdy building that can withstand any storm that comes.

Except the LORD build the house, they labour in vain that build it: except the LORD keep the city, the watchman waketh but in vain.

PSALM 127:1

Dwell in Unity

Lord, help me to dwell with others in unity. Show me how to be a part of a peaceful body of people who follow You. Let me not to want my own way all the time, but for the sake of unity choose to let others share their thoughts and ideas also. Help me to cultivate a spirit of unity wherever I go. Amen.

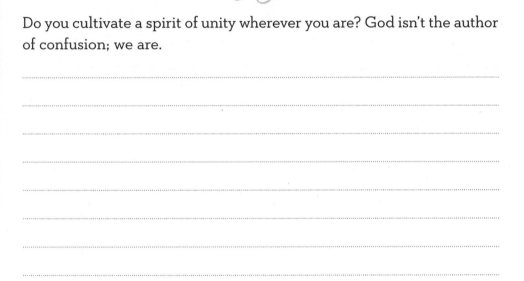

Do you cultivate a spirit of unity wherever you are? God isn't the author of confusion; we are.

Behold, how good and how pleasant it is for brethren to dwell together in unity! It is like the precious ointment upon the head, that ran down upon the beard, even Aaron's beard: that went down to the skirts of his garments; as the dew of Hermon, and as the dew that descended upon the mountains of Zion: for there the LORD *commanded the blessing, even life for evermore.*

PSALM 133:1–3

Search Me, Lord

God, You know me well, but I'm asking You to search my heart today. Look in all the cracks and crevices. See if there's anything that shouldn't be there. Check out my thoughts. Sometimes they come unbidden to my mind and I don't like what I'm thinking. Search out my ways; see if I need to repent or change something in my life. Cleanse me from every sin. Amen.

God is the best heart specialist in the business. Ask Him to do an examination on your heart. He can find those things that might cause you to be spiritually diseased.

Search me, O God, and know my heart: try me, and know my thoughts: and see if there be any wicked way in me, and lead me in the way everlasting.

PSALM 139:23–24

Instruction and Knowledge

Lord, help me to have a teachable spirit. Don't let me think I know more than others. I know You can use anyone who is open to Your Spirit and obedient to Your voice. You used a donkey to speak to Balaam one time. If You can use a donkey, You can certainly use another person to teach me something. Give me a discerning spirit to know truth from error, and then let me be willing to hear someone else. Amen.

God can use anyone He pleases to carry out His work. Be careful of thinking people aren't qualified to be used of God. He does the qualifying, not man.

_____

_____

_____

_____

_____

_____

_____

_____

Apply thine heart unto instruction, and thine ears to the words of knowledge. . . . Buy the truth, and sell it not; also wisdom, and instruction, and understanding.
PROVERBS 23:12, 23

Watch and Be Sober

Jesus, Paul admonished the Thessalonian Christians to watch and be sober so they would be ready for Your coming. I want to be ready also. Don't let me be caught up in the darkness of the world around me. You have given me light. Help me to walk in that light so I will be watching and ready when You return. Don't let me fall asleep spiritually. Amen.

Are you watching for Jesus to return, or have you fallen asleep spiritually?

_____

_____

_____

_____

_____

_____

_____

_____

_____

But ye, brethren, are not in darkness, that that day should overtake you as a thief. Ye are all the children of light, and the children of the day: we are not of the night, nor of darkness. Therefore let us not sleep, as do others; but let us watch and be sober.

1 THESSALONIANS 5:4–6

Ask for Wisdom

Lord, You told us in Your Word that we can ask for wisdom if we need it. I do need wisdom in my life. I want to make good decisions, speak wisely when I open my mouth, and know what direction I should take in life. I want to know how to live in harmony with those around me. All of these things take wisdom. Please give me wisdom. Amen.

Everyone needs wisdom in their life. We all have many decisions to make. God knows this, and He has offered to supply us with wisdom. Ask Him for it.

_____

_____

_____

_____

_____

_____

_____

_____

_____

_____

If any of you lack wisdom, let him ask of God, that giveth to all men liberally, and upbraideth not; and it shall be given him.

JAMES 1:5

Peace and Holiness

God, Your Word instructs me to follow peace with all men and to live a holy life. Sometimes that's hard, but I want to do as Your Word tells me I should. Help me to be a peacemaker. Teach me how to live a holy life. My heart's desire is to see You one day. Without holiness, I know that's not possible. Guide me into a life that pursues peace and embraces holiness. Amen.

Peace is sometimes hard to come by, especially if someone rubs us the wrong way. God's love enables us to love the unlovable and to pursue peace with them. It's a part of living a holy life.

Follow peace with all men, and holiness, without which no man shall see the Lord: looking diligently lest any man fail of the grace of God; lest any root of bitterness springing up trouble you, and thereby many be defiled.

HEBREWS 12:14–15

SCRIPTURE INDEX

NEW TESTAMENT

Matthew

ENCOURAGING AND PRACTICAL
JOURNALS FOR YOUR QUIET TIME

The 5-Minute Prayer Plan Journal for Women

Many Christians yearn for a dynamic prayer life, but we often get stuck in a repetitive routine of prayer. This practical and inspirational journal will give you new ways to approach prayer with 90 focused 5-minute plans for your daily quiet time. These prayer plans explore a variety of life themes appropriate for women of all ages.

Spiral Bound / 978-1-64352-506-8 / $9.99

Morning by Morning Devotional Journal

For more than 150 years, *Morning by Morning* has provided readers encouragement, challenge, and thought-provoking insight from the pen of one of history's most beloved preachers, Charles H. Spurgeon. This fantastic journal edition of Spurgeon's bestselling daily devotional contains the complete, original daily text.

Hardback / 978-1-64352-539-6 / $24.99

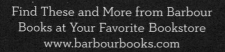